The Loser's Gospel

Elijah Ellis

Published by Elijah Ellis, 2024.

THE LOSER'S GOSPEL

First edition. February 27, 2024.

ISBN: 979-8224307418

Written by Elijah Ellis.

Table of Contents

The Loser's Gospel

A Note

Seven ideas conjured, 4 practiced, and none succeeded. If you ever find this book, that means this was greenlit by my supervisor. You'll find out who that is when you continue to read this collection of thoughts. If you, the one reading, ever decide to write a book...it's a lot of writing. I used to tell myself, "Your first idea is your worst idea." Looking back on that, I'm still right. There's never any real purpose behind what you write for the first time. It's just a bunch of words that somehow form a sentence you understand. Then you look back and realize that the randomness of letters means nothing compared to what it used to. Writing in the moment is fun at first. You have all of these ideas just soaring through your mind. All racing at imaginable speeds to reach your heart. After typing so many words I realized that every idea sucked because it raced to a void in my heart. So why am I writing this book that has a very specific title? I'll be honest, I don't know. I tried so many times and never really felt anything. So I decided to do something I should've done long ago. I turned to God and asked him what I should do. There are people I wish I could talk to but am afraid to. Family, friends, and even enemies. I have a hard time speaking to others. Now you, my dear reader, may have already scoffed at the fact that I turned to God for this. To that, I say, "Oh well." It's a sad reality but many people do not love God. Even Christians in the age I live in don't love him like they say they do. It's like seeing a relationship where one partner abuses the other in their own unique way and gets mad when challenged. I don't say this with pride. I used to be like that. It's painful to know that you were no different from them. After a lot of setbacks, I figured out what I needed to do. I asked God what I should do...he told me to write. I'll be honest, I was doubtful at first. But even now I realize that if I have such a personal and powerful being by my side, there is nothing that will fail. I guess I can say that my reason for writing this is to apologize to God for doubting him so much. I sometimes envy those who can recognize their spiritual gifts and submit them to God. I struggle with that. This isn't me wallowing in self-pity. Nor is it some scholarly argument for the existence and morality of God. This is my declaration to the world that I am a Child of God and what has come as a result of it. It's more like a long letter to God and the world. To be honest, I'm giving personal convictions and revelations I have come to accept. Not to say that what I believe isn't biblical. What I am saying is that this man was made differently. The perspective God has given me may be different from others. But it has helped me grow and reach others. This is how God affected me...

Note: Throughout this book, I will be using the term Christian (obviously). To clear up any miscommunication between us, I will give you a simple definition. Christian, as I will use it, simply means a follower of Christ. I do not point to any denominations ever. I do not specify how devout someone is with the word or the world. If I need to specify, I will do it. Otherwise, "Christ-follower" should be what pops in your head when I use the word. Now that we have that settled...

The Inheritance of Sin

Before God made me, he decided that I should have a certain amount of melanin in my skin. Not too much and not too little. Just enough to make me, Elijah Ellis. I was born from a family that was somewhat Christian. You'll see what I mean later on. My name was originally going to be Isaiah for some reason. But someone thought that my name should be Elijah. The name is biblical of course. But not many know that it originally was Hebrew. It means, "Yahweh is God." I used to think I was like every other baby, crying to breathe in air that they never have before. Apparently, I was more...quiet, like a corpse. This could've been a sign of my intrinsic weirdness or it could've been a sign of a battle for my life. A battle that was won by the one who wanted me alive.

Like most people, I have no clear recollection of what happened between the ages of zero to five. I remember some things like the toys I played with, shows I watched, certain events, and a specific trip we went on. But out of those vague memories lies a dream I had that I'll never forget. As I was sleeping, I woke up in my bed unable to move. At the foot of my bed, several fleshly puppets started dancing in weird ways and singing. I couldn't do anything but watch as the room started quaking from their violent dancing. Then I woke up, relieved that the nightmare was over...Or so I thought. I woke up in another dream, and they followed me to it. They mocked me as they continued to violently shake the room I was stuck in. Then, at some point, I woke up...and the vague life I lived continued until I was five.

Everyone has a time in their life when they remember becoming aware of everything. Their consciousness peaks and becomes aware that it does exist. At this point we know how to make sentences that sound good to us. I woke up that day being aware of my birthday. June 4...my birthday. Everyone recognized that it was my day to live. A day that belonged to me and only me. The day was mine to relish in. And at this time, there was no chaos to pay attention to. It was pure innocence running through the fabric of my being like a stream of water rushing in a river. Innocence that was bound to be corrupted by that which is not truly understood.

Sin is one of those powers and a very sensitive topic for many people within my generation. When someone who isn't Christian or a miseducated Christian hears something about sin, they usually turn a deaf ear. Part of the reason, from a Christian perspective, is because people love sin. The human heart is incapable of following God's law. More specifically, his wisdom is what they cannot understand. There is a whole lot of truth behind this. Not everyone likes murder but most people love violence or hatred. Not everyone likes sexual abuse but most like sexual exploitation (I promise this'll make sense later). Another reason people hate talking about sin is more personal: Judgment. A very famous statement that is shot around a lot, regardless of religious affiliation, is this: "You shouldn't judge others." Now I could go on a 100-page tangent about the hypocrisy behind this sentiment but I'll hold back for now. What most people really mean is this: "You shouldn't judge me." This doesn't just mean the person, but everything they connect themselves to. If you gossip about someone they hate, they'll join in. But if you gossip about someone they care about, they will intervene on their behalf. There is almost this natural guilt we have that we project onto others. People hate feeling like they can't belong somewhere. The creatures known as humans are complex in many ways. We think we understand the next person, only to find out that the same person has layers and layers of uniqueness to them. Human beings have desires and feelings that they feel need to be expressed. Every human is like a carefully crafted piece of art that the artist spends meticulous time perfecting. Sin is like someone coming in and ruining the art piece called "Human." The word comes from the idea of "missing the mark." When I use the phrase 'inheritance of sin,' I'm referring to the splatter of black paint that dripped down from Adam all the way down to the rest of humanity. So while some have more black than others, we all have black infecting the deepest parts of our being.

Weirdly enough, it seems like people understand the sacred nature of humans. They believe their desires to be good, regardless of what others think. The problem is not the desire itself but the root of it. The root cause of our desires comes from a lie as old as humans: That we can do it ourselves. "You don't need God, you can be like him." From the heart, sin is born. It seems that we have forgotten that life flows from the heart. Satan never directly lied to Adam and Eve. In a twisted sense, he told the truth. They did know good and evil and they did not die. Some have made the grave error of interpreting this part of Genesis as proof of God being weak or stupid, not realizing that they have fallen for the same trap. Satan never cared about Adam and Eve prospering. He never cared about the knowledge they would receive. His main goal seemed to be this: To get Adam and Eve to question the goodness of God. Once he got them to question God's authority, he won. He was able to drag a piece of creation into darkness. Adam and Eve both knew that The Tree of Knowing Good and Evil was forbidden. It was when the thought of God's goodness was challenged that they then saw the fruit of that tree to be good. What immediately followed was not a literal death. They didn't die on the spot, but they did separate themselves from the source of all life, which is no different from death. There was also something else that followed: Shame. Their nakedness was not for us to believe that the state of nudity in modern society is good. It is proof that we are created by God. The state of nakedness is a very vulnerable, very uncomfortable condition to be in. Regardless of how often it happens, it is not a state that people want to be in constantly. It is very much possible that this secret shame felt by nakedness is us subconsciously saying to God, "You didn't make me right." That reminder of what you were born with can be weird to think about. So how do we respond to the question of who we are? We clothe ourselves with what exists in God's world, just like Adam and Eve. Either that statement sparked a revelation or you are still confused. I'll simplify it like this: The human condition of sin was and still is caused by challenging God, which leads us to use his world to craft for ourselves what we want ourselves to be. This isn't me saying that people want to be addicts, hateful, promiscuous or criminals. I won't place all the blame on humanity but a good chunk of responsibility is there regardless. The phrase "free will" probably popped into your head. It doesn't just mean that we, humans, can choose whether we want to love God. It also means something else: The possibility of the world going wrong has always existed since the beginning. Now before you close the book and call me a heretic or go online to prove how evil God is, I must say this: The reason that the condition of the world was like that is because love is best experienced in the freedom to choose. Now I will do something uncomfortable for myself: Share a testimony. It isn't me saying, "Here is this very specific moment in time that I believe God was trying to talk to me and I listened." It's like me taking my clothes off in front of you. Not for anything weird of course. But for you to see the scars of sin and how this piece of work named "Elijah Ellis" was and is being restored from black paint.

Evil Infected Children

Children are praised for their innocence. Their carefree nature and their strange ways of exploring things around them. They're ignorant of a world that hates them. I was no different from them. Trying desperately to grasp onto the feelings that came with the four-stage cycle of earth. With fall, the crunching of leaves produced a sound that can only be described as "orange." A chill that isn't too cold but not hot enough for your hair to keep you completely safe. The smell of pumpkin and cinnamon approached as every night produced a unique song that no man could ever create. Halloween and Thanksgiving were holidays to be excited for. Candy for one and bottomless food for the other. With winter, the snapping cold against your face can only be described as "white." The layers of clothes my mother made me wear kept me cozy even within the classroom where the cold could not strike. Winter brought snow and Christmas, a holiday we made for giving and receiving material goods. Me and my brother would wake up six to seven-o-clock in the morning rushing over with excitement to see what those strangely wrapped boxes had in store. I remember one Christmas where I got a game that I played for the entire day when I had the chance. After Christmas came the reset of the calendar into a new year. After that was Valentines, a remembrance of love shared between couples...at least if you have a couple stray dollars to spend and someone to spend it on. Whether or not a relationship ended did not matter to Earth, for her next season was approaching. Spring brought new life and colors. But the main feeling of that season was "green." Bees were common all over and animals we couldn't see before were becoming more active after what we thought was a long slumber. New life brought new joy. And new joy brought a new sense of freedom that summer would carry. With summer, the heat of the sun blasted down creating a feeling that can only be described as "yellow." Everyone was out of school. No more assignments and no more tests. No more math and no more reading. The waters of pools and oceans beckoned to us to jump in and splash around as if eternity was already here. There was just one unnoticed problem...evil was still there.

Evil isn't as outgoing as the stories we saw and read as kids would make it seem. Evil prowls around like a tiger. You never see it until it strikes. Sometimes, it will team up with you to enact its will. This corruption starts when we are children. Children, while innocent, can be mean and ruthless. There are certain phases within a child's life that most parents I've seen seem to dread and relate to. Those phases of rebellion, selfishness, and just overall mischievousness. Of course, this doesn't mean I blame children. That would be stupid. If you've ever had a younger cousin, you know what I mean. Jesus loved children, that's why he died for them. He knew that sin would affect them somehow. He knew that he had to bear the responsibility of what sin has done to humans. All are dirty, and they need to be cleaned. But our eyes, especially when we are young, are blinded by the dirt of a dark world.

With me, I was one of the more "peculiar" kids. As long as I remember, I had a very strong imagination. I was one who dreamed every single day. Whether I dreamed at night or during the day, I was going to dream of something. My dreams came with the desire to share them with others. I don't remember many of the kids accepting my dreams. Not to say that they hated me, but that they didn't understand the words only I could understand. But there were kids who accepted my dreams. I remember a time in second grade where I liked a girl. Everyone knows how childhood crushes are. It's the first time your body reacts in a way that your parents never taught you. Feelings that mere words cannot explain at the time. The school this took place at used to be a high school. If I were to go back I would see that. There was even a track field there. On that track field is where it took place.

We were running around the track for PE and I noticed her from a distance. To this day I'll never understand what went through my mind at the time. I ran up to her and slowed down to her pace and shyly expressed how pretty she was...and then ran off like the wind. I honestly don't remember what happened after that besides her becoming my "girlfriend." We all know how this went...good for the most part. But like a lot of things in this world, they must end. When I expressed my dream to her, she accepted it. But we all have to wake up at some point. Just like the other friends I made in that school, I hardly saw them after. They had to wake up from the dream I shared with them, while I stayed asleep. The more I dreamed, the more I thought. The more I thought, the more curiosity dug its way into me. At some point, I was introduced to the concept of sex. It was the first time the seed of evil planted itself into me. Whether this interfered with my friendships I'll never know. But one thing is certain...I never stopped dreaming. Not every dream was one of bliss. Dreams are visions. And no one else can see your visions. My own mind became a weapon used against me. Everyone knows that verse that claims: "No weapon formed against you shall prosper." For some amount of time, it did prosper. It was the beginning of a kind of suffering that isn't taken as seriously as it should. Mental anguish took a hold of this dear child and made him suffer ever so slowly. My days were filled with a kind of torment that words could do no justice for. The more friends I began to lose, the more the truth of a cruel world crept into my mind. And how convenient it was that I had to switch school districts right before I went to middle school. I remember so vividly how much scarier the night sky became.

Middle school is the strangest period for growing humans. It is when we become more defiant to authority. Whether it be our parents, teachers, morals, or the law. I'm no stranger to darkness. It was at this point that the curiosity surrounding sexual activities grew. Some might say this is a good thing, that I would be able to explore my sexuality and how it operates. I hate that thought and everything about it. I hate that I had this curiosity. It led me to pornography, which eventually led into masturbation, which led to a deep-rooted addiction. A madness that people support. If I never found God I would probably praise sex workers and those who lead a path of lust for others to taste for themselves. But I cannot see my life and how lust affected it and say that these things are good. Everything about that world is disgusting in ways that I don't want to talk about. I would go as far as to say that these institutions should be destroyed. Is porn and sex the central problem of my life? No, not by a long shot. It is one of many parasites. One of many seeds within my psyche that would change the way I think.

The Loser Grows

I said before that I don't put the whole blame of someone's condition on them. I do believe now that there were many spirits at work against me. When I look back on my life and reflect on things that happened, it seems too perfect to be called a coincidence of events. Though many deny the existence of spirits, it doesn't seem foolish to believe them. Even outside of scripture, it seems strange to believe that there isn't some force tempting us. Sometimes I look at history and wonder how certain events happened. I don't mean it literally, as in the chronological sequence of life. I mean it in a more uncanny sense. The Trans-Atlantic Slave Trade is a good example. How could someone go through several loopholes of logic to come to the conclusion that not only a person of a different skin color is inferior, but that they are nothing more than property for a race who sees themselves as superior? And how could they use scripture to justify it? It seems a bit too perfect at times that such evils in history existed and continue to exist. Almost as if the people behind it are more like puppets to a will they can't understand. Even on a personal level, this seems to be true. Either way, it is no coincidence that my life turned out the way it did today.

The start of middle school was fun. I remember making lots of friends from a game that they considered difficult at the time. I wanted to test their assumptions and see just how hard the game was. To my surprise, it wasn't easy but it wasn't difficult...with the exception of two levels. To their surprise, I became the first to complete these levels. But that was when I found out that the levels I beat were only part of a demo for the full game. I convinced my mom to get me the game. After months I beat all of the levels. Within those months I made a lot of friends amongst the boys and girls. For once I felt as if my dream was being shared all around. But there was something that happened within that school year...I was struck by the horrific truth that is death.

Before coming to this new school, I had a dog. Her name was "Tiny." Not the adjective I would use. You wouldn't think that if you met her in real life. I'll never forget the cornchip stench of that dog as I walked into the room we mostly kept her in. I'll never forget about the time she came over to comfort me as I bawled my eyes out seeing my mom finally return home from wherever she went. And I'll never forget the heaviness that weighed in on my heart when it came to hearing the news about her death. A death that happened before I even knew it. I spent that evening trying to come to terms with the fact that she is gone. I went through the stages of grief, but I never really recovered. Evil had planted another seed into my heart through the death of my friend. A friend who was there for only about three years, the longest friendship I had. I remember I spent days crying because of how I treated her sometimes. I didn't know how to love her and neither did anyone in my family at the time. We just did. Love is an emotion born from God, not us. Love is not something that anyone can truly explain. There are too many layers to love that one culture can never get right. The Greeks used different words to describe different kinds of love. Love has different ways of expressing itself, that much is true. And sometimes, those expressions are selfish, hurtful, or unnatural. God loves too. And while his expressions of love may be confusing or downright hurtful from our perspective, they make sense in the larger context. God expressed his love through his justice among other things. When Israel sinned, he had to do something about it. To let someone you love just live any kind of way is not love. God also expressed his love through his kindness. After Elijah the prophet ran away, he prayed to God to kill him. But God did not answer this request. Instead, he gave Elijah something to eat and drink and let him rest, for he knew that Elijah's job was not done. However, he couldn't just overwork a faithful servant. He knew his body needed a break and so he gave it to him. The Greeks weren't completely wrong. You wouldn't have sex with a family member like you would your marriage partner. That would be incest, not love. But to treat them differently because you believe one love is so vastly different or better is foolish. Love is more like a tree with many fruits. Each fruit is a different expression of love itself. But as I said before, humans are corrupted by forces beyond their control. So are these fruits, regardless of their taste, actually good? Anyone is capable of love. We feel it all the time. We search for it constantly. We know that deep down we just want love. But we enact certain desires from that exhausting search for love. Sometimes we find it. And when our love is taken away from us...where do we go? That is the question that has haunted me. For it was at this moment that an emotion I had never considered before stirred within me...hatred.

Hatred is similar to love in that it can be expressed in different ways. It isn't the opposite of love. If love is like a tree, hatred is like a cancer that creates new growths when it can. What some consider karma is just hatred that had no outlet before. My hatred was nothing new. I remember a time where this bus of kids all made fun of me for no real reason. They were just jerks to me. That was the first time I ever felt hatred in my life. It wouldn't last forever though. I told my mom and she made me change buses. The love she had for me made her realize that getting to my stop quicker should not cost me any amount of joy. It was better to have a longer trip than to suffer. But the love of a mother was not enough to quell the hatred of a lost child. Among other things, I started to hate my father. There was love, but my hatred drowned it. The way he treated my mom made me angry. And for years I believed she was a victim. I only saw one side of the story. It wasn't just her who was abused. It was both of them, victims and perpetrators of a cruel world. Being part of a family that didn't know how to love because they didn't know how to love God only added to a darkness they couldn't see. I remember being forced to go to church every Sunday when my mom was recommended a new church by one of her friends.

When I think about it now, I'm glad she did. She found a church that was true to what scripture said. Regardless, it ruined my weekends when she made us wake up early. At some point, it just stopped. I don't know why, it just did. For me personally, I wouldn't consider my experience religious trauma. I was just secretly hateful of things. Some may call it indoctrination. I would hope those people never teach their children any of their morals or ideologies. Even considering how young I was, I played a part in my perspective of the church. To say that a belief is bad based on a personal experience isn't fair. If that kind of logic creates racist, sexist, or homophobic mindsets, why is it okay for specific cases? But I didn't know this. I didn't know that my perspective about God would make me secretly hate him. But within that hatred, I still wanted heaven...because of how much I was afraid of hell. That's another expression of hatred...fear. Fear helps you avoid what you hate. If you hate spiders, then fear will help you avoid them. If you hate snakes, fear will help you avoid them. If you hate people, fear will definitely help you avoid them.

After Tiny died, my life spiraled into madness and disarray. I remember how the colorful feelings of seasons became more boring and uninteresting. Everything became more gray. Having to move to another middle school didn't make things better but worse. After struggling through the last bit of sixth grade, I got the news of having to go to a new school again. Going to that school with a developing porn addiction only served to ruin my dreams even more. It was at this time that I gained a lot of weight that was unknown to me. And that weight would make me an inevitable target for the sinful nature of kids my age at the time. When I first went to that school, I realized that most people were already friends with each other. New kids only get attention when they have things other kids are attracted to. At this point, I had nothing. And I was to be someone who had no one to talk to. This isolation lasted for weeks. Although I had online friends that I still talk to and play games with to this day, it doesn't fill the spot of someone physically being there for you. And every night I pleasured myself for a reason I never knew. Somehow, I was able to interject in a conversation one day and made friends. The number of friends I had grew...or so I thought. There were people who genuinely cared for me and there were those who only talked to me because they knew my strange nature in a world of sin would give them entertainment somehow. I never knew just how cruel the world really was. To top things off, I was made fun of for aspects of my life. Whether it be my weight, my personality, or my grades. No one knows the true weight that depression drags in your life. Even someone like me didn't understand the depression in the lives of other people. I remember one specific moment in seventh grade that used to piss me off every time I thought about it. We had a substitute in one class and a conversation about sports was brought up. I'm not a fan of sports. The only things I was a fan of at the time were video games and anime. But being a black man, it seemed like blasphemy within my culture to not like sports. I can only assume that something within me wanted to point out the bullshit they called culture. I made a comment and the whole class seemed to get angry at me, including the teacher. How was I supposed to know why the entire class gave me scornful looks when I mentioned my distaste within the world of sports? I already live in a culture that decides what you like and what you do based on flimsy aspects of your life that we call "identity." Was I to assume that their darkness piercing my heart was a result of teasing? Or would it be better to assume something different? One could say that I shouldn't have assumed at all. That's easier said than done when life shows you different. Whatever the case may be, I was more upset that day than I already was at life itself. For this day taught me that the world will hate you when you are different and there is only one way to survive: Fit into a crowd never meant for you.

As the days progressed further into the years, I realized that I was quite behind on assignments. I didn't really care though. At this point, I was hoping that something would take me in my sleep. That something would kill me and end the miserable existence I lived. The only thing that kept me from suicide was the fear of hell. Was hell really worth ending the pain of one world? Heaven was the only hope I had. To be in paradise and avoid eternal suffering was the only gospel I was taught by those around me. But at the time, I didn't exactly know the feelings I had. And one conference between my mom and the other teachers proved that. They caved in on my weaknesses, showing me just how much I was failing in school. And here in America, failing in school is failing in life. I was lucky that one specific teacher wasn't there. An English teacher. I hated her class and damn near everything in it. How ironic that literature has become a passion since then. Even though she wasn't there, the others shared her concern. I call it concern because truthfully, they did care enough to be angry at me. Maybe they saw some kind of potential in my worm-like life that I couldn't. Or maybe they didn't want to see me ever again. In any case, there was a question about what I was doing during the class time given to all students. I answered with a smirk, "thinking." It wasn't a lie, far from it. It was the pure truth at hand. I was always one to daydream. Even writing this now I will have moments of just spacing out and returning to reality as if it never happened. My daydreams are specific enough to deserve their own book. But this book is about something different. One day I will make that book. However, there was one pervading thought that always struck me every single day: "When will I go home?" Not to the house I stayed at but to the mansion Christ said he saved for his believers in the sky. Though I knew nothing of these homes, I knew that this world that I lived in was only temporary, like most things...including my laziness in school.

Sometime within the second semester of eighth grade, I found out about Track-and-Field. A culmination of activities I knew nothing about. I don't remember who sparked the idea specifically, but I do remember seeing the flier for my school's track team and being drawn to it. Despite my weight and lack of athletic abilities, I decided to try out. It went as bad as you could imagine. One of the first events was a 400-meter run, the entire track for one lap. I could barely run 100 meters and they expected me to run four times that amount. Regardless, I ran with strength that couldn't have been mine. Some other girls mocked me as they saw me attempting to do what they considered impossible. I consider this a moment where God had his hand in a sinner's life. Most of us were taught that God hates sinners. That he would leave them to die at the hands of their foolishness. That he would only give blessings to those he considered "Holy." But the true gospel speaks differently. The gospel of Jesus Christ explains that he came not for the righteous but for sinners. Consequently, every human is a sinner because of their inheritance of it. Every human is almost destined to follow the temptations of the devil and his army over God's word. We all deserve to die, that's why God did it for us. Here's a visual for what that hand did: God secretly put a fishing hook on my metaphorical shirt and slowly...very lightly tugged at me. I would feel an inclination towards certain desires and actions that led me to Christ. But I didn't know this at the time. All I knew was that I was far from my goal. I wanted to give up at some point...but God didn't let me. He told my feet to step, even when it hurt. He told my heart to beat, even when it hurt. He told my mouth to breathe, even when it hurt. He told my spirit not to give up, even when it hurt. And before I knew it, I was at the end of the line. The coach told me I would do shot put or discus. He wasn't sly...I knew it was because of my weight. You wouldn't make the big kid run. But that isn't where Track-and -Field ended. It was only the beginning of something good. A journey of weight loss...but it was not with that school team. I got cut because of my grades...Yeah, I expected something different too.

Somewhere before those tryouts I went to see a doctor for whatever reason. Only thing from the visit I remember was that I was, what I'll call, "primed" for diabetes. In layman's terms: If I didn't get my shit together, I would have diabetes. That thought stuck with me during my weightloss journey, which is not as easy as people make it. I didn't want to not do track, so I went to a recreational track team in my town. It was one of the worst things I've been through. Not only did we have to run most of the practice, but we ended all of that torture with another 400-meter sprint. I wanted to give up somewhere on the field. But one of the coaches wouldn't allow it. He did something unexpected. Instead of screaming at me to continue, he started a conversation while running with me. I entertained the conversation and...I made it. I told myself I wouldn't go back. My lungs felt a pain more dry than the school tryouts. But where my body wanted to give up, something else didn't. The next few days were canceled due to weather. Oddly enough, I wanted to go back. Despite all of that, which I considered torture, I wanted to do it again. Every day we would warm up with two laps around the track. It was hard at first, but it got more fun as time progressed.

Though I was not in shape to be running, something about it was somewhat liberating. It wasn't the air becoming wind or the motion of your feet exploding with energy to fuel your next step forward. The idea of continuous but slightly drifting motion allowed my mind to dream in a way that it never dreamed before. It dreamed with consistency. I don't mean consistency in the sense of thoughts being clear and understandable. I mean consistency as in one thought at a time instead of multiple at once. The ocean of madness experienced calms. It was a feeling I never understood until later on in my life. The only problem with running on this team was that I was not built to run. I was built to throw according to the head coach. He wasn't wrong and I wasn't mad. We made a subconscious agreement of what my role on the team would be. To be fair, I was pretty good at it. Me and this other guy had a similar role on the team.

I made a friend on the team that I would talk to every practice. He and I went to the same school. I'd say that he was one of the first witnesses of the step that became a journey in my life. He saw me change in various ways. I tried a new hairstyle, became somewhat more social, and deconstructed my feelings for the first girl my developing body fell in love with.

Oh yeah...that's a detail I forgot to mention...I developed feelings for a girl. Not a simple crush either. It felt different. I would say I became infatuated with my lust for her. One day, at the end of my last period sometime in the winter, I had to switch seats with someone who was being "annoying" in the words of that specific teacher. I was somewhat upset because I really liked that seat. Changing seats somehow introduced me to what I considered one of the prettiest girls I've ever seen. Some wicked spirits decided that giving a porn-addicted, socially awkward, mentally ill black kid kindness that wasn't shown to him before was a great idea. It was great, just not for me. The smile she radiated when all I did was offer to take her book made me feel a sensation greater than when my mom smiled at me when I was a child. I wasn't like the other boys at the time. I wouldn't say I was feminine in nature. I just didn't do or enjoy what they did. I had boyish tendencies but my existence was different. This isn't me bragging about it either. Even now I sometimes get annoyed at the fact that I am so different. That my sense of humor, tendencies, and overall life feel inferior. My difference made me feel more cursed than anything. Even the friends I made over a game console knew as such. So for someone to see my difference and smile at it with such warmness made my heart skip beats every time I talked to her. At least that's what my mind conjured. A fantasy I fell in love with. It was a love short-lived. It was not meant to be the story of how a loser got to date one of the prettiest girls in school. That is reserved for fiction. This is how the loser was shown a reality that everyone said was true.

Sometime during the school year, a new kid showed up. A boy specifically. And not just any typical new boy. A new boy that had that aura that attracted others to him instantly. He was what the girls called cute. Obviously, I was not that. And the girl I liked was one of the girls that called him cute. And he was a boy that would become attracted to her. Attracted to the point of becoming close to her. A closeness I never got to experience. A new seed was planted in me at this time. It was jealousy. A feeling that one has when their attachment to someone or something is threatened. I thought for once I could feel something more than what I felt when my eyes were trapped in the world of porn. But those kinds of relationships are reserved for those who chase after them. Those who work for these things, not for someone like me. There wasn't any other emotion born from this that wasn't hate. My unique nature was cursed by me. I thought to myself that day that if I wasn't so different, maybe I would be able to feel appreciated for being human. This school taught me that the only way to live the human experience of youth was to be human. It also taught me that who I was was far from human.

After my journey to forget the existence of a girl whose kindness planted a dark seed within me, I ventured off into the land of high school. This is where I would change. This is where I would become human. This is where I would prove that I am a man. I would be the presence there. I would be a kid to have sex with some "bad bitches," as they say. I would become popular and carve my name into the minds of those around me. I started this as soon as I could. Those who knew me would see my transformation and would talk about it as if I was a beautiful butterfly emerged from his cocoon crafted by an ugly worm. I did make a name for myself. I did talk to some people. I developed a crush but fumbled as any boy would. The first semester seemed to pave the way for a future full of the fulfilled desires my heart had. The Christmas break ended and new classes were upon us. What was English became math. What was History became Science. The pattern continued for classes. But my image wouldn't change. It would carry over into my next classes to grow stronger over time. That was until another girl appeared. And this time, it wasn't just a kind gesture or two. Some of my friends swore I was crazy for saying that this girl showed interest in me. Whatever the truth was, my mind decided to go the route of twisted love again. I was reminded of affection I was never shown before. Porn was enough of a distraction when I was told that it was not a sin. With no fear of hell, I could do what was considered sin and live in paradise. This girl did not drag me away from that dream but added to it. This is where the loser gets what he wants...right? Of course not. It wouldn't have crawled its way here if it were to be good. It was more of a prelude to true madness. This is what I would consider one of many "fumbles" in my life. When an open door is presented before you with promises inside, you walk in right? When you have an opportunity in front of you, there is no question of if you should walk through that door. But for some reason, I was afraid of that door. It was almost like the future me behind that door was screaming at me to never go through it. His voice was so loud every time I thought of talking to her. My heart would beat so hard that I could feel genuine fear rushing through my veins. It wasn't butterflies in my stomach. It was more like centipedes in my skin tearing into my stomach. And this fear lasted for longer than it should've. But every time I was ready to call it quits, a strange occurrence would have me believe a hope that never should have existed. A hope that led to madness. After some time passed, what I thought was a fascination towards my existence turned into a fascination towards someone else's existence. That thing I called jealousy returned. He talked and I didn't. He was strong and I was weak. He was not the Saul to my David. He was just himself and I was just me. That spark of jealousy that existed before resurfaced as a wildfire. A wildfire that used the fuel of other seeds to burn away any good within me.

Somewhere along the way, my dad introduced me to certain "truths" of Christianity and God. I can't blame him for what he taught me. Everyone wants to be right about something. And I was no exception. False prophets and teachers know that people yearn for answers to the more difficult questions. Questions about suffering, especially that which is counted in history, invoke one's body to go search. They soon find answers that satisfy their criteria. They share these answers with others as if they are true. When I was told of the idea of being a descendant of God's chosen people, I was fascinated by the idea. The concept of God putting me, a worm amongst men, above the others planted a seed of pride within me. Before I ventured down this path of madness, I put myself on a pedestal above others. "I don't sin like them, God. Bless me for being as righteous as your saints." I figured that even though I sinned sometimes, I was better because I was chosen. The color of my skin made me better than those who looked different. And because the girl of my dreams during my adventure in high school at this time was of the same people according to what my father said, I was stuck on the idea that she would be the one I married. But this isn't true. If it were, I wouldn't be writing this book, would I? I wouldn't sacrifice secrets to the world for the hope that someone sees God shine within me. I wouldn't know that the future ahead of me was one of madness.

How could such a loving god allow me to experience the breaking of my sanity at the hands of other humans and my own dreams? My mother, who still didn't understand how to truly love, must have noticed the breaking of my sanity against God at some point. Even before this incident, I used to question everything. My existence as a human within humanity sparked questions of all sorts. Questions about why I was born a male and destined to be so weak. Questions about whether or not I truly liked women sexually. Questions about my future. Questions about right and wrong. And when I learned what an answer was, I would consider that truth. I was born male because of chance. I had to like women even though the thoughts of other boys made me curious. My future was what I made within the confines of school. These are the answers I developed through my biased research. My mother saw a glimpse of this and decided that I should be a part of a speech and debate club. I joined, thinking my intellect would help me escape the feelings I had for the girl previously mentioned and a way to explain my dreams to other people. I met some people within that club I would consider friends. But there would be others I considered enemies as well. But none of them ever took me away from the fantasies my mind conjured about a woman who was already talking to someone else at the time. They may have already been dating, but I didn't know. I shared my dreams with these friends of mine and they called me insane after so many times. They weren't wrong, but I wouldn't accept it. My pride as someone chosen by God amongst others would not shatter at the hands of other sinners. What I thought was love for God became a twisted vision of what my dreams should look like. And no one has ever proved my dreams wrong. So anyone who spoke against them was nothing but a fool. If I said that being gay was wrong then it was. If I said sleeping around with others is wrong then it was. If I said making fun of me was wrong then it was. I became the judge for God in my dreams. And every debate I participated in only proved to God that my obsession with being right was born from the evil within my heart. At some point, it was like God had enough of my madness. Not because he hated me. Quite the opposite really. He loved me so much that he presented an opportunity to escape the hell that I created for myself. I asked her over social media if she was dating the one I considered an enemy. She answered plainly with a yes. Nothing more and nothing less. And where my dream was crushed, God saw an opportunity. As if my hand were possessed I wished them success. Success? For my enemies? Yes...and for some time I thought it to be an act of righteousness on my end. And more time after that, I finally accepted the reality presented to me: I am nobody...and I deserve nothing good, even if it is a gift. I was made to be tormented. I made friends in this chapter of my life. I even tried to do the funny thing where you fix your heartbreak with someone else's body. But I was no casanova. I was Elijah Ellis...a loser amongst men. Not all hope was lost though. I wouldn't find God. Quite the opposite actually. I found another sweet temptation presented by men who considered themselves tickets to success in this world. I found what they called, "The Red Pill."

Some have already cringed at this statement. The liberals would call this the Alt-right-pipeline. They believed this to be a predatory attack on young boys, like me at the time, to get them assimilated into the disgusting and hateful world of conservative politics (Ironically they are no better). But I didn't see it as that at the time. I saw it as a way to become what I was never seen as: Human. Where I was drawing at the time, they told me to do more of that. They told me to focus on money. They told me how women worked and what surefire techniques could get you closer to them. So close to becoming one flesh with them. And you wouldn't have to worry about any other consequences after that. Women had several means of birth control and men had an easy way known as the condom. The possibilities were limitless. "If I didn't care about women, they would care about me." That's what they taught me. The other big names of that so-called-pipeline also crossed my path. Things were going great for me. Then one day, a friend of mine decided to get me to "spit game" at a specific girl. I accepted his challenge happily and even succeeded in doing so. At some point I got her social media information and we chatted for a while. My only goal was to finally see what the hype about sex was about. But God had other plans for me. As if on cue, a certain plague occurred. Many of you know what I'm referring to. There were a lot of people excited about not having to go to school because of it. The temporary joy of being away from school for break during a period where we weren't supposed to be on break made everyone excited. Everyone thought that we would be able to relax and have fun going on vacations and hosting parties. But a plague has to be taken with caution. What was bliss at first turned into hell for most people. And within that hell I realized some truths about this person I was talking to. After some time I decided to never talk to her again. I was frustrated at first, but after some time I stopped caring. At this point, I started to build a barrier around my heart. Isolation allowed me to completely ignore myself. I could cry, but I would not know why. I could feel joy, but I would know how fickle it was. As if I didn't hate myself before, my hatred became the means to protect myself. But I wasn't done with this world. I still had a mission of sorts. "Before I die, I will show the world my hatred." It sounds corny at first, but that's truly what it was. It wasn't like I didn't have a reason to be angry. Most of my life has been a nightmare that I couldn't wake up from. Every part of my human experience only showed me just how shit life really is. Love was pointless. Every time I thought there was some hope for it, I would be met with confusion, mixed signals, madness, and just...hatred. This quarantine was the perfect time to further that vision I had for my life in this world.

During the quarantine I decided to do two things: Hone my artistic abilities and finally pave the way for one specific dream in my head. You see, this book was not the only thing I wanted to write. There was one specific dream about a specific set of characters that I've always wanted to tap into ever since the first one popped into my dreams. And on some day, I decided to write the first words of the story that had no real direction. Much like the life I was living at that time, there was no direction in the script. It was all over the place, just like my mind. Before I knew it, I lost all motivation to write. So I went back to drawing. And soon after doing that, I lost all motivation to draw. This cycle continued throughout the quarantine for everything I thought I loved to do. The scourge that I thought died with the madness I accumulated during the days of high school youth returned. Before I even knew it, depression had taken over my mind, bringing back that desire to die. Everything was taken from me. My youth was nothing but void promises of fleshly pleasures that never occurred. They said we would return to school by that summer if cases died down. But they kept rising. Homecoming and prom, events that I skipped before because of my inability to socialize with others, were taken when I thought of participating for once. My will to draw, write, live, and even dream...all taken away from me. I was nothing but a bag of flesh that only moved to release excrement and keep itself clean. Well...as clean as a depressed man can be. The days and nights passed by with barely any excitement for anything. Anything that brought some kind of joy died as quickly as it lived. And even though I considered myself a man of God, I was nothing but a hypocrite. I hated all kinds of people and things. And I never admitted it at the time, but I hated God as well. I was angry at everything that he let happen to me. Every time I prayed, nothing happened. It was as if I was destined to suffer for God's amusement, the same way we laugh at the suffering of others sometimes. I believed that I was just one giant joke for heaven to laugh at. I wish I knew how God felt about those thoughts...how hurt he must've been seeing what sin has done to someone he spent intimate time creating in my mother's womb. At some point, I had to wake up from this nightmare. But when would that happen? When would my own mind stop dreaming and wake up from its own madness...

God Cries Too

Maybe it's just me, but when I got older I started to sympathize more with my parents. It started as childlike love and turned into hatred and indifference. I used to think what would life be without them. To make a long story short: I thought it would be nice. I could respect them, like most kids my age did to their parents. I could say, "They did so much for me," or "I wouldn't be here without them." But I could never say that I loved my parents. In fact, I hated them. These feelings became more true to me as they got angry. Like most kids, I did not care when adults got angry. I always thought of them as not human. I always thought my parents were unreasonable. I dismissed their anger as if they were not even human to begin with. Even now, most people are incapable of seeing their parents as other humans. They see them as bags of flesh that should bend to their will. Anger seemed to be an emotion that adults wanted, not a consequence of seeing what they can't control. How much more disrespect do we show God? I used to think that the things God wanted were too much. I used to think that he ruled with a fist much stronger than iron. I believed that when God is angry, he takes the most unsensible, extreme actions. Everyone knows about God's anger against humans. It started with Adam and Eve and continued from nation to nation, tribe to tribe, family to family, and man to woman. But his anger is described in a unique way according to the Bible. It's easy to see God flood the earth and say that he was being extreme. Or see that he says homosexuality is wrong and believe that it is unloving. His anger is a result of his love for humans. That seems like a statement that contradicts itself right? It is if your definition of love only includes the positives and none of the negatives. One negative of love in this life is that it hurts. When we love people and see them doing certain things that we know will hurt them, we are inevitably hurt by the experience. We love them regardless, right? How much more do you think God loves humans? Would he really be loving if he didn't get angry at humanity? God faces challenges, a fact that we don't want to accept for some reason. Challenges in this case do not make God any less powerful. Quite the opposite actually. If God faces challenges with us and succeeds, then he is more powerful than what we think. Of course, we are talking about God here. We have to assume that this being is beyond our understanding in every aspect. However, we can get some kind of understanding. I believe that there are two concepts that help us understand the nuance behind his moments of anger: Omniscience and patience. Omniscience means "all-knowing." Patience is someone's capacity to tolerate something.

God's omniscience means that he knows everything. He knows about things that we would never truly understand. Trying to understand the infinite power of an infinite god is like trying to understand each individual cell of each individual organism that exists. It's impossible and pointless to what we need to understand. He knows everything about everything because he created it. So when he says something is bad, there is something about it that you may not truly be able to understand. Where one would question why God does not approve of premarital sex, God sees how sin has corrupted the human mind to view sex as a casual activity only meant to pleasure ourselves. The entire story of The Bible shows how sin corrupted every aspect of creation. This corruption exists in areas of our lives we don't consider. It doesn't just make us rebel against God. It makes us believe that we have better authority over the earth than God. And because God doesn't want the sinful ideas of humanity to take full hold of creation, he has to get angry. He doesn't want to hurt people or make us suffer. Job didn't suffer because God wanted to laugh at him. We never truly understand why he let Satan do that to him. But God didn't leave Job to die and say, "Worship me." He restored all that Job had lost by double. We think the universe operates by strict human principles. God says that it is different. We ought to listen to him. After all, he created it. Does he not have a right to get angry? If you spent time creating something like art or a business, wouldn't you be mad if someone came along and tried to destroy it? I would be concerned if the answer is no. Regardless, that thought should help you understand God's anger. His anger is a response to the chaos we want. Regardless of how small you think it is. Just like any painter would not want one drop of some foreign color on their piece. But God's first instance of anger was not something small. The first humans decided to listen to that cunning creature and tried to seize power and authority by their own rule. This is why Adam and Eve were kicked out of the Garden. However, God loved them so much that he said he would save them and their descendents from their mistake. His knowledge allows him to decide what is right and what is wrong. Just as you know the ins and outs of what you make, how much more would God know his own creation, of which you are one of. Everything God made was good, so anything apart from what is good is evil. Even more than that, the good creation can ruin his world. As I said before, true love can't exist without the freedom to choose. However, being sovereign over a world full of corrupted humans who believe their wisdom to be superior to God's wisdom is more complicated than one would expect.

Patience is not understood by many. We think that it has to last forever. Patience is a limit. If we run out of patience, why should God? He wouldn't be good if he didn't get angry, which means it has to happen. But the thing about God's patience is that it lasts a lot longer than we give credit for. God gives people lots of chances to turn from their ways and go to him in love. This seems counterintuitive, especially for my generation. We can look at events like American slavery or The Holocaust and immediately say that God is doing his job wrong. A hard-to-swallow pill for both of us is that the people who committed those atrocities are not so different from you and I. Of course our actions are different from theirs, but we are both humans right? So were they. If God judged us by the standard we judged them, we would be just as guilty. God loves everyone enough that he died for people who did not love him back to give them a choice to love him truly. This love is not limited to those who believe themselves to be good by the actions they do towards others. This love extends to the outcasts of society. To the evil one and the lame one. He gives them opportunities to turn away from their sins and let him clean their bodies of the evil that sticks to them like tar. He won't judge people unfairly. Hell is a place made for Satan and his angels because they don't want to be with God. So those who are sent to hell are those who want to be away from God. This isn't to say that those who've rejected God previously are subject to hell no matter what. Quite the opposite actually. I was one who rejected God and followed the god my heart created for me. And yet, he welcomed me with open arms after years of rejecting him. All have fallen short of the glory of God, so all have rejected God and his good wisdom at some point in their lives. Where we cast those away who cheat on us in relationships, God is different. No matter how much we sin, he is so loving to the point of chasing us down, waiting for us to hear his call. Incidents like the flood and the plagues of Egypt are because of people directly rejecting God after so many times. They were not people that knew nothing of God. Noah preached to those in his day and Moses showed Pharaoh the power of God himself many times. At some point, God gets angry and does something about the evil being done to his creation. But even so, he took responsibility for us.

Some time during quarantine, I decided to speak to God truthfully for the first time. I knew things and even decided to read the Bible myself (If you're curious, I got burnt out around 1 Kings). However, I practiced New Age spirituality alongside it. I wanted things of the world to be mine. I listened to the tarot cards and the universe. It actually worked for some time. Only a couple of months. Remember before when I said that my desire to create died? That's the reason why?

Manifestation theory most definitely works. But once the wolf comes to ravage the sheep that is your soul, you are left to die. The universe doesn't care for you or I. That's what I learned at least. After all of that I decided to see what God wanted. I spoke to him and recalled my entire life until that specific day of November of 2020. I then decided that maybe, just maybe, I should actually give him my life for who he is despite the life I lived. And for some reason, even after saying I didn't regret any of it...I cried. I cried tears that I never have before. They weren't little drops of water that made your nose slightly stuffy. These were tears that made your nose cry as well. I never understood what this meant. But some time before writing this I realized what it was: It was me feeling what God has been feeling for some time. I cried because he was crying with me. Finally, I answered the call of the one true God. The Lord of Lords, Jesus Christ, had called my name before I ever knew him...and I answered the call. It was the gospel that saved this loser...that showed me that I was not that. I was a human, made in his image. And from that point on, what I heard quoted from scripture before became true. But it wasn't instantaneous. It was a journey that continues even now writing this book. I didn't share sensitive information to make you pity me. I shared this information to show just how good God is. For now it is my wish that the world sings, "God is good," and that all of creation sings with them.

The Steps of a New Creature

That night was the ultimate proof that God loved me. It's different from just recognizing he exists. The gospel of John has a very well known verse that every Christian knows. "For God so loved the world that he gave his only begotten son, that whosoever believes in him, shall not perish, but have everlasting life." There's actually a lot more to unpack from this verse and guess what? We don't have to dive into ancient language to discover what it means. I promise that the title of this chapter correlates with this verse. Let's start from the beginning of this simple sentence.

The first part of the verse expresses a sentiment that God has for the world. The word used is love. This part can be very contradictory to other passages in scripture when viewed with certain skepticism. It's difficult to explain how God loves the world with all the stuff he has done. Flooding the earth, raining fire on Sodom and Gomorrah, exile from the Garden of Eden, and much more. Luckily, there is one metaphor we can use to better understand the hard-to-grasp concepts of God's love. A concept that has become severely corrupted and misunderstood: Fatherly love. Throughout scripture, God is described with fatherly attributes. In this society, masculinity has words like 'provider,' 'protector,' and 'leader' attributed to it. (I have a lot to say about that but let's save it for later) Take these attributes and crank them up beyond their capabilities with man and you have an idea of what the Biblical authors were trying to say. This is why God might seem so violent in the Old Testament. It isn't something he wants to do but must, a sacrifice I believe many fathers can relate to. Disciplining a child, from observation, looks difficult. Even when it comes to my little cousins or siblings, it seems difficult. Their feelings are pretty fragile at that age. Getting a firm tone of voice with them when they seem so happy can be difficult depending on the situation. So how much more would God have to intervene when humans let evil run rampant in his world. They may be having fun and experiencing pleasure, but how can a good father love his creation and allow them to destroy themselves. We think children are fragile, but adults are fragile too. The difference is that adults break differently. It might sound like I'm saying God destroys humans before they destroy themselves. Just to be clear, I'm not saying that. Would a good father let evil overtake his children? How much more good is God?

The next part to analyze is the son. There isn't much to say here that hasn't already been said by others or myself. To give a brief explanation I'll say this: Jesus is God. There are places throughout scripture that give context clues pointing to Christ being God. My favorite of these is that he is the only begotten son of God. There are other places throughout scripture where The Sons of God are mentioned. We, humans, are even called children of God. What makes us different is that Jesus is the only "begotten" son of God. This means that, unlike us, he shares in the nature and deity of God. He is God. Humans beget humans. God, begets God. I like the translation that uses this word because it gives a better understanding of who Christ is. What's interesting about the son is that most people, not excluding me, have had some kind of idea about him that was wrong. We think of conquering from the human perspective. We think of love from the human perspective. We think of death from the human perspective. Even how we think of Jesus is from the human perspective. We forget that God became human. So he knows the human perspective quite well. The world has its own way of living. Jesus, the son of God, flipped the script. This world was given to him. That same world killed him. But three days later, he rose from the jaws of death and conquered the world. "Why would God become a mere human?" Because you and I couldn't do what needed to be done for the rest of the world.

The next part to examine is believing. What does believing in God actually mean? Some people think that it means acknowledging the existence of God. Though it is part of the truth, it is only a fraction of it. It requires more. To have belief is not just an intellectual task. It is something that requires your whole being. Some say that it is blind devotion. To them I would say that belief, no matter the subject, requires evidence. You don't believe what you don't have some kind of evidence for. Even if that evidence isn't good evidence, you still believe it. Everyone believes in something that can't be fully proven. An opinion is a belief that has evidence behind it. This subjective reality points to something else. We believe a conclusion that evidence points to, not the evidence itself. We believe a chair will hold our weight based on the evidence provided by science and experience. We believe that our political leaders suck because of evidence provided by the media and personal experience. Even more, we Christians believe in Christ because of the evidence provided by his life, death, and resurrection. I won't explain the evidence. It's out there for you to find. Plus, I don't want to bore you with unnecessary pages. All you need to know is that believing in something is a lot more than just blind devotion based on feeling. The belief in Christ as The Son of God leads to the final part of this famous scripture.

Eternal life, the ultimate reward for Christians, what does it mean? The final part of this verse gets taken out of context a lot. Most Christians believe eternal life to be something that is received after death. This is one of the many misconceptions that corrupted Christianity presents. Eternal life is something that we can receive right now. Yes, that means that at this very moment, where your eyes are tracking each word within the present flow of time, you can receive the gift of eternal life. The best part about it is that you don't need a PHD in theology to see how I came to this conclusion. It's said by Christ himself. "This is eternal life: that they may know you, the one true God and the one you have sent–Jesus Christ."

Now here's the truth about that scripture: It's hard. It sounds easy on the surface. But if anyone believes that going from a life born and molded by sin to one with God, who considers some of our deepest desires as evil, is easy...I want the confidence you have in yourself. If I knew that being in a relationship with God was this hard, I would have ran away from him just a little longer. There's a reason the title of this chapter has "new steps" in it. Every single moment that you walk with God will lead you into something that will reveal the darkest abominations of your heart. I've had the displeasure of seeing mine and continuing to see them while writing this. The next few chapters will be my unnecessarily extensive observations and theories about the human condition supported by scripture. These observations come from personal experiences with myself and certain kinds of people I have met since my journey with Christ started. Each second experiencing some of the most strange scenarios and people has helped further my understanding of this world. Any man or woman or child that tells you that you can stay as you are as a Christian is a liar. Being a Christian makes you a new you that is better beyond your imagination. It becomes clear what true eternal life gives us. It doesn't mean a boring life with no fulfillment. It is the exact opposite. Christianity exposes the human heart by challenging it against what God says. Many will try to say that their way of Christianity is better than the other. Whether it be because they know more about scripture or that their god allows for a multitude of people within their church, it doesn't matter. We are to be like Jesus, not use him to create a new ideology. If the steps of your walk of faith do not change you, you are not following Christ. It is not enough to just say, "I'm not perfect." Christ died so that through him, you could be made perfect. I'm not the one who called us new creatures. If you make the claim that you are a follower of Christ, then you must accept that everything about you needs to change. Regardless of what it is. It may sound harsh, but it's more of an investment. It's like paying $100 to get $1,000,000 in return. What makes this better is that you don't need to pay or do anything. God makes the effort and all you have to do is trust him. Of course, that ain't easy. Nothing about it is easy. But if it came so easy, it wouldn't be good. Especially if what we're talking about is our existence as humans. I've shown you the wounds. You have an image of the blood spilled from them. I think it's time to see the experience after the fact. For the next couple chapters, I will show you the extent to which God has made me new. How my old ways continue to die even today...

My sexuality

I'll start with this because I know someone was curious enough to jump here. Yes, I did question my sexuality before this. I never actually tried to prove the confusion true or false physically with others. I was taught that such thoughts were evil and would send me to hell. And if I ever did enact upon those thoughts, I would be irredeemable according to those around me. Some might pity me for not being able to explore because of what I was taught. Sure, I didn't get the freedom to explore my curiosity about other boys at the time my body was primed with curiosity surrounding sex, but I don't regret it. I don't need the pity of anyone for a past that is dead to me. If you believe that I am not as free as you, that's fine. It's weird how someone can judge another human's life based on what they believe to be true about their desires. This curiosity was a temptation that would never truly be enacted outside of my dreams. And even within my dreams I tried to contain such thoughts, only for my heart to scream at me. It's funny how the human heart works, at least my own. At one moment, I'm feeling nothing but hatred towards homosexuals. The next moment I'm feeling deep compassion for them. Compassion, not in the sense that I believe their lifestyle to be aligned with God's will, but compassion as in a longing to reach out to them. It seems condescending but believe me it isn't. Once you learn the truth, it's hard to go back. Seeing people reject the light and base their existence on sexual desire is a tragedy that I have become fascinated by. As if the desire for sexual intimacy is not temporary like a passing wind. The understanding about sex and sexuality I have gained was not meant for me to pride myself in knowledge of the confusion that is sexual desire. It is a means to hopefully bring people to a closer relationship with God. But in order to do that, it must be said that most people's views on love and sex have been warped and perverted since they were children.

I'm not going to make the argument that every lesbian woman or gay man has been abused sexually as a child, that isn't the whole truth. I will say that most children have been shown some kind of twisted view on sex that made them believe certain things about themselves and others. Regardless of sexual orientation, corruption has infected a child. I was unfortunate enough to be one of those victims. I was introduced to the concept of sex through porn. Though I didn't exactly watch porn after that, I was curious about what I discovered. An aspect of the world was now added to my dreams. This dream brewed more curiosity about the female body within me. That curiosity soon became desire as I decided to venture into that world for myself. That world showed me a kind of affection that I never was shown before. Though it was my own body pleasuring itself, I felt the comfort of knowing that I couldn't leave myself and I would always be there for myself. I made friends that were always separated from me in some kind of way, drifting apart from my life. And the best friends I've made over the game are people I could never see with my own eyes. Knowing this fact made me lonely. But porn and society taught me that sex was a way to connect with someone. To reach that high point of intimacy would help me connect to those I could never connect to. I was never able to pour that desire into anyone. I was never really close with people. Not from what I can remember at least. The harsh truth of reality is that the intimacy you create through casual sex is nothing more than you exploiting another human for personal gain. The lust I carried for other women was born from the twisted dreams that conjured from a developing porn addiction. It told me that women were nothing more than bags of flesh to carry my sexual desires. I knew I was ok to lust for women because society said it. Both men and women made that reality become more of a truth. Though not so easily seen, sexual exploitation was everywhere I looked. From someone's slightest glance at a girl's ass, wondering about the feeling of it against their skin, to the pinnacle of sexual exploitation: abuse. The acts are different, no doubt about that. However, there is something to be said about the fact that the core desire is messed up. The desire to take another human being as your own and use them to fulfill your own desires. I was no different. The desire against girls soon turned into a curiosity against boys. For some time, this part always confused me. At some point, the idea of "gayness" started to creep its way in my head. I never told people about this because of the fear that I would be shunned just like the others. Part of me understood that no matter how much you tried to be human, once people found out about your sexual preferences, the only thing you were was the label they slapped on your face. I didn't want to be a gay man. Hell, I didn't even want to be a straight man. I just wanted silence. If there were a way to rip that part of me out of my face, I would've already done it. But life isn't so simple to where you can just get rid of temptations.

It didn't help that I wasn't the most masculine fella at the time. Roughhousing, cars and trucks, sports, the whole nine yards of American masculinity wasn't my cup of tea (Trust me I will get to that conversation soon, I promise). I wasn't the most boyish guy. I wasn't a feminine fellow though. I danced between the fine line of identity. What made it worse was that I was and still am black. Sexuality is one of the many toxins infecting the people of my community. Sexual exploitation is just as bad here as anywhere else. Coercion, threats, violence, gaslighting, and just a whole host of other things that are done against men and women just to get one more moment of sexual bliss. The objectification of humans produces these symptoms. Adding the idea that you must have certain experiences in your life in order to be human, (Or in this my case, Black) it's easy to see why I would have such a problem with it. Would I be writing this section if I did have some kind of sexual experience? I know I would. The only difference would be that I would have a heart heavy with guilt knowing that someone God created was exploited for my temporary pleasure and possibly driven further away from Christ. I could imagine how every word of this chapter would make me nauseous. I took something good, a human, and ruined their image all for the sake of pleasure that is easily forgotten. That's what happens every time you go back to watching porn. You further the exploitation of humans. If you ever take the time to research what the porn industry actually does and how it affects viewers and actors/participants, you'll be questioning why people like it so much. It produces a kind of thought that continues to make humans less human. The moans of "pleasure" you hear are not real. They are responses to a kind of abuse. Sure, they may like what they are experiencing, but they were trained to think that way. Those who support porn in any capacity are participating in a madness that spreads like cancer. That's what I have been recovering from: Madness about sex.

Every time I ventured back into that crooked world of pornography, the idea of being a bisexual always pervaded my twisted dreams alongside it. I never understood why that was the case. Maybe there was a wicked spirit that heard my parents or some other family member gossiping about that kind of lifestyle. Or maybe it had something to do with the little interactions I had with other boys. I was introverted, but even introverts want friends. I imagined all kinds of erotic fantasies...but those that even considered having another man I forced into some kind of subconscious box. I considered my sexuality set-and-stone. I liked women and nothing would convince me otherwise. That's what I kept telling myself. If I ever accidentally saw a thumbnail of gay porn, I would make myself forget I ever saw it and tell myself that I was on a mission. A mission to prove that my mind never could swing that way. This already mangled dream turned into hatred for those who practiced homosexuality. The disgust I had towards my body turned into hatred for others. It couldn't just be contained for myself. It had to break out and manifest in some kind of form. It wasn't until I was shown true love that the hatred that wrapped around my heart became weaker and weaker. It soon died off, after a long process. What was hatred became an uncanny compassion towards that I hated. God had turned something evil into something good. He did something that no man could ever do. People could make the argument that I should have never had such feelings in the first place. Or maybe, I should have just explored the bodies of others. Men and women alike should have tasted my lust. I, of course, have a huge problem with both arguments. Sometimes, when I looked at the media containing Queer people, two voices would speak. One voice would be annoyed that the stories of my time contained anything dealing with queerness. The other voice seemed to be more sympathetic in nature. As if it were telling me just how tragic the life they live is. The bullying, shaming, outcasting, judging, and general hatefulness that they go through seemed to pervade my body as well. As if I could relate to these individuals. "Do they hate themselves?" A question that my subconscious would ask. The questioning of God and sexuality started to appear again. I stopped questioning myself and turned to him for answers. It was then that I found something...

I found several videos from all kinds of people saying that God affirms these kinds of relationships. This raised more than just my right eyebrow. It seemed that those who took lifetimes to translate the Christian scriptures made one severe error. The word "homosexual" never existed in the Bible. Even more, the scriptures that mention homosexuality are those that talk of violent relationships or pedophilia depending on who said it. This baffled me. And though part of me wanted to just accept what they said as truth, something else said to see it for myself. So I decided to see for myself what they were talking about. The first time I did my round of research I asked about homosexuality in the Bible. Multiple websites conflicted with the idea that God condemned such actions and vice versa. It was at this point that many would stop and claim that this is the truth. But something told me to dig deeper. I went into both languages that talk about this issue, Hebrew and Greek. I went to several websites to translate certain words and see what they meant. Was Paul specifically talking to pedophiles and abusive partners? Was Moses talking about those who abuse children? My skepticism would not allow me to accept what they gave me as the truth. I then turned to the actual book itself. If they got only this one specific thing wrong, surely everything else was wrong. After so much time I realized something...I realized that the issue wasn't about who was attracted to who. Yes, it is a sin to be gay...but it is also a sin to be straight. What do I mean? Before I get into that, I want you to have this thought on a backburner in your mind: Why is it that when people argue this, they only go to specific verses? Those for and against it. They only go to where it talks about sexuality and nowhere else. Now I can begin. There are aspects of this topic that are not talked about enough. It isn't just an issue of sexual desire. Identity is one of the many things that plays a part in this. Before writing this, I looked at videos of people who used to be gay turned Christian. I saw a mixture of comments under these videos. There were other Christians congratulating them on their revival in Jesus. But others did not share the same joy. They would question how they could follow such a cruel god who wouldn't let them be free in their sexual desires. They would mock their beliefs and make it seem as if they were fucked in the head. They would call them traitors to their hearts. They would say that they were never gay to begin with. Before I would laugh at them and say, "Woe to the fools who mock the children of God," as I rotted away in a chair. But something told me that it was more than that. They wanted love and they wanted to not be judged for who they are. These people had no true identity before this. They didn't know who they were before they leaned into their hearts desires. They were mocked and outcasted for their dreams. I wasn't the only kid with dreams. They had dreams too and were mocked for it. Sin told these people that they are what the world tells them they are.

That they are their sexual desires. That the desire for the pinnacle of intimacy and acceptance is what their lives will forever be based on. They were just like me at one point...and I am not someone who should kick them while they are down. It is written that our enemy is never another human. There are dark powers at work behind every human that contributes to evil. They are no different. The Devil tells one side that their sexual desires are everything and the other that they are a waste of oxygen in God's world. God told me that I should reach my hand out and grab theirs to lift them up. Not saying that I am some kind of savior. Rather that the power given by the one who saved me can save them. I don't have any doubt that God can reach them. But that doesn't mean I shouldn't act for him. Despite being taught lies by wolves dressed in sheep's clothing, God still chases after them. False prophets and teachers gave them hope in a gospel that says, "Live how you want," instead of a gospel that says, "Be free and live better than how you are." That's why many cling on to what those hypocrites told me. These people wanted to be known and heard, not punished. There was a gospel that only preached of hell and its eternal suffering. They were one of the main targets of this gospel. They are not any more evil than the next person. All have spat in God's face. Some do it through abstinence of sex and some do it through the abuse of it. Regardless of what kind of sex you have had that broke God's standard for it, you can be washed by the blood of Christ. I do not and will never have a heavy heart to say what is right and wrong, but I will forever apologize to God for contributing to the corruption in them. I can't reach them all, but there are many who need the truth. And this is one of the many ways the truth will be revealed: From God, to a man who never had sex, been in a relationship, or even successfully flirted with a woman. How strange it is that this man could have such conversations and thoughts... But what even makes sexual immorality immoral? It must first be established what humanity was made to be. I've heard people say that humans are sexual beings. With every fiber of my being, I disagree with this argument. We may have sexual desires but they are only part of the equation. And I don't agree with the idea that having sexual desires as part of our being or us reproducing sexually makes us sexual beings. Our whole lives are not (And shouldn't be) dedicated to sex in any capacity. This is clear within the story of humanity's creation in Genesis. Adam and Eve were created as "Living Beings." That phrase may not seem important because of how we think about the term "living." We just think about living as existence before death. I propose an idea that this term of living correlates to what God meant when he told Adam and Eve that they would die. Genesis states that God breathed the breath of life into man and made him a living being. Humans had a very special purpose in God's world: To experience God's love and to share that love with others. Have you noticed the connection? We are not sexual beings because of sexual desires. Rather, sexual desire is one of the many proofs of what we are: Living Beings. We have senses, emotions, desires, and goals. But even these concepts that are grand to us only serve to point at the bigger picture. An art piece is not judged by the details alone but how the creator put those details together. Even if we don't see it at first, every detail within a piece of art speaks to us something about the creator and the world it exists in. Remember what I said about sin previously? We are all like individual pieces of art that God spent intimate time creating. If every part of our being was made to be loved and to share that love in some kind of way, then our sexual desires must have a specific design and purpose. That is the part that so many people miss. Sex is good, not because of what it is but because of who made it. I could go into the fact that sex is how humans create more of themselves but it only scratches the surface. There's a mystery about sex that always rings the bell of confusion in my head. That mystery is pleasure. The act of sex is pleasurable for at least one person. I'm surprised that I don't see more people asking questions about the pleasures of sex. Even amongst Christians I believe it should be discussed. Not to excite the lusts within someones' heart, but to see how it points to Christ. What about the sexuality within us was worth God's time to be created? There's some things within scripture that answer parts of this question bluntly and parts that are just confusing. For the more straightforward answers, the Bible presents these claims: Sex is to be had in the confines of a heterosexual, monogamous marriage. Sex is to be done in private. Sex is an act of submission. These facts give a clear purpose for sex: An act of intimacy shared between two lovers who are male and female within the confines of their relationship. So sexual immorality would be anything that goes against this purpose, right? Of course...What other answer would you expect? The more confusing parts of sexuality are those that are more personal to us? It is those questions that go against what God has made. "Why does it feel so good if it is so bad?" "Why would God make me this way if he didn't want me to do this?" Or anything that questions sex that isn't so explicitly said in scripture. One of those things we think we have to "interpret." A task that many (myself included) do not like doing. There have been many wrong interpretations of the mystery of sex. Not everyone can be right on this subject so someone has to be wrong when it comes to interpretation of truth. I don't claim to know everything. I do claim to know that God knows everything. Based on that truth I can make an assumption about these mysteries of sex and sexual desire: They point to Christ by revealing our sinful nature. Remember that Satan's deception caused Adam and Eve to question God's word. They started to think that he may have been wrong about the Tree of Knowing Good and Evil. When they took that fruit, based on the desire that it was good to eat, they soon felt shame. Let's apply this personally: Those who grew up around church-folk may have heard the idea that sex before marriage was sinful or certain acts of sex were bad. Once they got older, they began to question God's word when it came to sex. They decide to taste the fruits of sex, whether it be through actual sex with someone or through some kind of pornography. From there, they gain information about a world they could never understand. This develops into a form of guilt or shame. After that, they search within the world for things to "cover themselves up." Just like how Adam and Eve needed clothes to subdue the shame they felt from their decision. Even worse, they tried to hide from God. Similarly, we try to hide from God through the manifestation of our desires. I'll go deeper into that later. For now, part of the mystery that is sex points to God even within our sin. Our sinful nature points to a perfect being that created what we use for ourselves. In the society I live in, it has been cranked up to a degree never seen before. Sure, gay lovers existed at all points of human history. But none of them have used sexual desire in this way. What makes LGBT+ seem like such a blessing for our society isn't based on the freedom of expression, but the community that allows for identity to be found. It is like a second family beyond what we are given. What's more is that the LGBT+ is not the only facet of sexual identity. Though it has no actual name, American society has become a cancer of lust for people. The liberation of sexual desires and acts has paved the way for folks to have a false identity in a cruel world. The only issue is that it isn't much in the grand scheme of things. Life is more than sexual urges, is it not? There's so many other good things out there. To have sexuality be such a pivotal part of your life only serves to trap you in another kind of prison. If being in the closet is one kind of prison, coming out is going to another. The only difference is that this prison is more like a field where a rope is wrapped around your neck to keep you from going too far. This isn't me trying to say anyone who has their sexuality close to their heart is inferior in any kind of way. I'm saying that there is more potential in humans than what they confine themselves to. It is a fact that idolatry is worship of what is created instead of the creator. Sexual immorality is worshiping sex as a god and treating it according to what you believe is true. For there is a purpose for sex that is infinitely more good and pleasing than what the constricting box that is sexuality says. It may seem like I'm trying to soften the blow right now and trust me,

I'm not. I know how personal sexuality is for a lot of people. I've had my fair share of encounters that have opened my eyes to the experience more. And at the time I never realized it, but it was almost like I was experiencing what Jesus did with the adulteress. I could easily say how they are on a path to hell, but what good does that do? Instead, I will expand on the words that Christ said to that woman after saying he wouldn't condemn her: "Go and sin no more."

The adulteress was identified based on her adultery. Like many of us, we believe subconsciously what people say about us, especially ourselves. We internalize it and make it reality. However, when we are faced with the truth, we have nothing to say. Our shameful acts are thrown out for everyone to bear witness. And there might be people who try to have punishment acted against you by an outside source. However, Christ did not look at the woman and see an adulteress. Rather he saw a woman who committed adultery. This points to what Christ came to do. He came to redeem humanity. And humanity is not humanity without individual humans. He saw the individual who was being shunned by others, possibly even herself, and gave her a new life. "Go and sin no more." The phrase, when applied to our sexual lives, means two things: We can have sex the proper way, as God intended. And, we don't have to live based on our sexual desire. Of course, no one is forced to take the path that God gives. And I can see why someone wouldn't. It's hard to let go of something you held on so dearly to for a large chunk of your life. However, the act of holding on might be the very reason you suffer internally, without even knowing. The best thing to do sometimes is to just let go. We don't have to live according to our lusts anymore. The uncontrollable feelings we get for sex are not something we have to obey. In Christ, there is no sexual identity. We will still be creatures with sexual desires and that's ok. It is God who gave us sexual desire. It is only fair to give it back to him so he can make it better for us. And every time we feel an urge for sex, we don't have to succumb to it. Sexual desire speaks to a desire deeper within us:

intimacy. We long to love and be loved. All of our needs are met when we give our lives to God, for he created us to live in his presence. Sex is not the pinnacle of life or intimacy. It is one of the many fruits of love that is shared by a man and woman who love each other romantically. And those who have sexual desires for the same sex are not less valuable in the eyes of God. We were bought with a price. God gave his life for us. He spent years and years and years making the way for Jesus to come into the world and renew all of creation, including you. There is an idea my friend presented to me one time when sharing the gospel to a girl on campus. "When Jesus was on that cross, he thought of you." If we are to say that Christ died for us, is it not safe to assume that this sentiment is true? For all the sexually immoral, there is good news: You don't have to live within the confines of your desires anymore.

This is why I make the declaration that I am not straight or gay. I am not and will never be what man or woman says I am. God made me in his image but sin corrupted it. I have since been restored, and you can too. God made sex, sin corrupted it. We are to honor God with our sexual desires. Marriage is a sacred union between man and woman. Sex is meant to be had within its confines. Whatever deviates from that is what God considers evil. This doesn't mean that you can't be saved from sin. Remember, this is good news. Good news that a better life lies ahead when God is the center of it...

My Humanity

If you know me in real life (Which sucks for my desire to work from the shadows) then there is one undeniable fact about me: I am weird...and a nerd. This isn't just me saying I have a peculiar personality. I do...but that isn't the full story. I am genuinely a weird person, I will admit. From my taste in music, to my choice in words, to what I like to draw, and even philosophy (If you couldn't tell that part). I even had a phase where I was heavily invested in maggots. They may be gross creatures, but there was something so peculiar about how they live that made me draw worms and worm-like shapes for some time. To the average person, that's disgusting. And to be honest, they have every right to be grossed out by something like that. I still find worms and any other creature like them to be icky. In case you're wondering, my phase at the time of writing this book is spiritual obsessions. Things like ghosts, spiritual powers, demons, and stuff like that. I still love God, don't get any other idea, but there's something to be said about this. There is a certain mystery at work here. And I'll be honest here: It's very confusing to put into words.

Trying to describe everything about humanity from the lens of a human is like a chicken describing everything about its existence. It's practically impossible to come up with concrete answers for the human experience. All throughout human history, there have been myths and tales describing what life is and how to live it. Ancient Hebrews offered a strange conclusion to the answer of humans. They believed that humanity was a product of God's desire for creation and how it should operate. Apparently, humans were something God wanted to make and cherish. The pinnacle of his creation was us. When we talk about how God made us, we tend to only focus on what we understand. Three things come to mind here for me. The first is physical appearance. The second is personality. The third is human desires and our relationship to them. This makes us believe that God contributes to every portion of our lives. Part of that sentiment is true. I've said before that God made us with desires. I've also said that sin corrupts our humanity. I already explored one aspect when it came to sexuality. Here I want to go over some other ones that won't be as expansive as sexuality but equally as important. They all tie into one main struggle with life: Who we are.

The first thing is purpose. Humans in this day seem to enjoy describing themselves as it pertains to their purpose, or at least what they think their purpose is. Most people will say something about how their purpose is happiness, the wellbeing of their neighbor, or something within the world we live in. It is no surprise that the question of purpose is one that every human has had. Many believe that they have the answer to that question.

It's interesting to think that creatures within a world they barely understand can believe they have the answers to life's greatest questions. Should we trust the other with what our purpose is? Should we even trust ourselves? I don't think we should. Truth is something that is tested against lies and made triumphant. It takes multiple people to find the truth of something. Whether that something is physical, philosophical, or spiritual. But even a group of people can lie. Conspiracy is popular not because it's true, but because it is the regurgitation of someone else's thoughts that make sense. The evidence they present proves their madness. The point I'm making is that purpose is a calling higher than what man has to say. In order to actually understand purpose you have to accept this fact: Truth is simple. This doesn't mean that there aren't complexities in truthful claims, but the fact in itself is simple. For example: The sky is blue. There is nothing more or less about that statement. There may be a whole process with light and light reflection/refraction that occurs, but it all comes to the same conclusion. How much more, then, is the truth to what our purpose as humans is. I won't give answers. Just think about the idea first before coming to conclusions. I believe that you will be surprised at what you find.

Life is the next thing important to humans. I don't mean the things that people think make life worth living. I mean the constant motion of our existence throughout time. The past, present, and future. This isn't going to be me making an answer for the concept of life, just me observing it through my perspective. We try to put meaning into life. Some say that not doing certain things means you haven't lived life to the fullest. Of course, I will talk about them later. But to name a few examples we have: Sex, parties, drugs, relationships, and religion. There are many more things that I don't have enough time for. I have a point to make and taking my sweet time with them would only over-saturate this book. What I said before applies here though. Humans believe that they can decide what is and isn't true. So many people try to put meaning into things within life that we forget something very important: We wake up every day. If you are reading this, that means you are alive.

This brings me to the next thing that is important to humans: Death. Death is a truth so simple that it is scary. Death is the end of life. Death is an unfortunate fate that we all have to face. No matter who you are or what you do, you share the same fate as everyone you love and hate. Some live their lives in fear of death. They wish to not regret anything in life before they die. It is a strange way to cope with the truth of death. There isn't much to say. There is no formula for immortality. We may have lived longer than our ancestors, but all we did was delay the inevitable. The best thing to do with death is to accept it. To live life based on death is not a life worth living. Living for the things in life that truly matter doesn't help us not regret our life, but it makes the truth of death bearable. Fearing death isn't dumb. It makes sense why one would fear death.

Love is the next thing. Love is one of those things that is hard to describe. It's easy to experience but hard to dissect. Love isn't the nervous feelings you get when you see someone else. Love isn't the attraction to one's personality. Love isn't sticking through until the end regardless of challenges that face you. Like I said before, they're more like fruits. It's a reaction that happens because of love. There seems to be a kind of love that has all of these aspects within it: Romantic relationships. It encompasses all of those fruits into one person. It's a culmination of different feelings and desires. But it isn't the only love to exist. Love between friends and family is also part of our lives. And for the Christian, love for those you hate is also a thing. Some think love is pointless. Some try to run from it. Others chase it. We all have had an experience with love before. But what if we got the whole formula wrong? It's very possible that while we experience love, we go about it wrong. For example: You have a crush on someone and you get to know them. You two text each other and conversation is going well. They reply fast, engage, all of the vain expectations we have for people. Suddenly, they stop texting you, or their behavior is weird. One explanation that most people run to is that they lost interest. While this could be true, I have two things to say about that. Firstly, you should be happy if that's the case. That means that they never saw you as human, but an object of lust (Don't pride yourself. There's a fat chance that you are doing the exact same thing). Lust is temporary. Love isn't. That leads to my second point. It could very well be that their humanity is showing and they are afraid of it. What I mean is that they felt comfortable at first because they didn't have much to think about. But at some point, we start to realize that people we want to be with have to see our most vulnerable spots. That's scary. Love is scary. And how humans express their love can be scary too. I don't claim to be an expert in any kind of love (Lord knows I am everything except that), but what if we got it wrong? What if we are trying to force ourselves to experience something that we have no concrete idea of? Love is an experience that every human craves. It is almost as if our existence needs to be loved. In the world I live in, heartbreak seems to creep into everyone's heart somehow. Single or engaged, isolated or surrounded, religious or not religious. Regardless of who you are, heartbreak exists. And whether it is love, death, success, or failure that brings it does not matter. We have no control over fate. Does this mean that love is pointless? God forbid it is. Love is what drives us to live. We shouldn't hide from the inevitable, but face it. And the one thing that everyone will inevitably face in this life, regardless of how you define it, is love. So why do I bring this up in the first place? Before I became a Christian, I had no real sense of what any of these things meant. I only knew of their existence, just like everyone else. I live in an era that says that hard work is the key to success. That in order to live, to be human, you must work for something. While I do acknowledge that other views of humanity exist within America, this was the general view of things. "Chase the bag," as they would say. Before I heard God's voice, I was beginning to participate within that hustle culture. I even worked through some burnouts just to prove that I can be successful, that I was someone. It would be easy for me to say that humans base their life, identity, and faith on what is physical. Part of that is true. But the spiritual world is being intertwined with it as well. That means that our humanity is based on something beyond our understanding. Concepts that have only been scratched. There are people who exist in this world that believe they have sacred knowledge. Not just conspiracies, but even simple things. They believe that they are the gods of you, me, and themselves. They craft their vision of the world based on what they believe to be truth. They find some obscure knowledge and proclaim themselves to be smarter than us. They don't care about you and if they are gods, they suck at their job. There are even Christians who do this. Christians who believe that they are special in the eyes of God. They will never outright say it, but their words and actions contradict what they say they believe. For example, there is a sect of modern

Christianity that only cares about heaven. What I mean is that these Christians care more about the rewards that God will give instead of him. They are blind to their own pride because they use scripture to support it. It's very likely that you have seen it practiced or practiced it yourself. They are the hypocrites Christ was referring to. There's two types. The first one is what I call, "New Age Christians."The political term would be "progressive." I personally wouldn't use that term because they are regressing away from what God was trying to save them from. They are vulgar, lustful, judgmental, hateful, jealous, and lazy. They care not what scripture has to say but what part of scripture makes their hearts jump with glee. They can't see heaven because they don't want to. These are the ones who twist scripture to suit their carnal desires for paradise, both temporary and eternal. They aren't the only ones. The second kind of modern Christian just as dangerous. Some people call them "Evangelicals." The political term is Conservative. I call them The Old Age Christians. The same adjectives I used for the New Age Christians apply to them as well, just differently. They too only care for heaven, their personal reward, but in a different way. They care about what used to be. "The old is better than the new." They care more about tradition than The Kingdom of Heaven. They are more easily recognizable because of their outward hatred. The image in your head might be a White Christian who hates gays, promiscuity, parties, and the whole lot of american degeneracy while practicing very "strict" religious rituals within life. That's a stereotype of course, but there's some truth to it. You'll usually hear this kind of Christian reference scripture in some capacity without full knowledge of context. For example: That one verse in Corinthians that talks about those who will not inherit the Kingdom of God. I won't go into details, but it is a verse that is thrown around a lot. My point isn't about who will go and who will not. My point is that most people who use this verse maliciously do not care to read more. If they did, they would see the next part that says, "Such were some of you..." They care more about their image of righteousness than the will of God. They see the world as a battlefield where humans are the enemy and not hostages. I bring these examples to say that I tasted each one of these, for a lack of better words, shit ideas. Once I finally realized God's will for my life, being human became that much easier.

The truth of what it means to be human is a statement that made my mind go blank when I first heard it. It's easy to believe that we must take this difficult path towards truth and purpose. We are either a collection of molecules trying to pass their information on within a dying universe, or gods with a purpose more grand than we can imagine. Both extremes for this spectrum require too much. Now, you might expect me to say something like, "The truth lies in the middle of the spectrum." You're almost right. More like it doesn't even exist on that spectrum. What I have noticed about the Christian story is something so simple that understanding it is difficult. We, humans, are like machines. Every machine needs some kind of fuel to function properly. Give it no fuel and it won't work. Give it the wrong fuel and it will operate contrary to what you desire for it. The machine known as man is meant to be fueled by the spirit of God.

In order to make sense of what that means, we need to go to the beginning. There, in Genesis, we see something I mentioned before: The creation of man. I said in that part that we are living beings. But there's something before this that is mentioned. God "breathed" life into us. If you take a deep breath, you feel a rejuvenating feeling. That feeling is then breathed out into the atmosphere. That breath, regardless of how spiritual or literal you view it, is yours. Now let's take this concept and see how it can apply here. God breathes in, his energy becoming great. He then breathes out, into man, letting that energy out into the world. Or rather, I should say, into man. This is what gave man life. God's life brought humans to a state that they could not be in if he never breathed into them. Before I continue, I want to present a question you should think about: What is the spirit? I don't mean a specific spirit, but the general idea of it. If you have any kind of thought about it, it probably has this quality: It is inside of us. With that in mind, we can finally get to what the spirit of God is. Or rather, who is the Holy Spirit?

The Holy Spirit is described as God's personal presence. Can I tell you a secret? I don't think that's enough of the picture. And it's never going to be. We aren't meant to grasp the full knowledge of God's existence. He didn't give us the brain capacity to do so. I agree with the statement, but I don't agree that it is the whole answer. We use our mere experiences as humans to build a connection to what happens in the divine, and God is no exception. The Holy Trinity, for example, is man's way of explaining who God is. There are many who believe that the Trinity is a contradiction to scripture. However, I am someone who believes differently. If God is beyond our comprehension, who are we to say that he is only one person and not more? Still one God, but in a way that would separate him from the other gods. There are many instances throughout scripture where the Trinity is hinted at. But I'm not here to argue, I'm here to explain why one should even care about God's personal presence. Well, to put it simply: It's what makes us human. We are beings made to experience God's love. We have spirits. Parts of us that experience God's breath, which fuels our being. In a weird way, accepting the spirit of God allows us to become more human. I wish I could explain this great mystery, but I can't. I can't find the words to explain how God's spirit enabled me to tap more into my creative talents or how I became more of who I am now. I can give this example though: At some point in time, I hated my creativity. I was not proud of the work I made. I surrendered that part of myself to him, expecting him to destroy it and give me something else. Instead, he gave it back to me the next day in a way that surprised me. It was better than I could imagine. Ideas started flowing within and I drew more things. Life started to look different. And regardless of what tragedy fell upon me, whether it was physical or mental, the world never lost a shred of its beauty. It was as if Heaven itself was here. And it wasn't until this very moment, writing this, that I realized that the very feeling of heaven being on earth was not just a mere experience. It was a genuine reality that happened. I'd be lying if I said it was easy to understand that. So allow me to explore why it is so hard.

In the previous chapter, I mentioned something about how Adam and Eve put on clothes to cover themselves up. Their nakedness made them shameful, and their shame made them put on clothes. Take this metaphorically please. I will not be held responsible if anyone who reads this part goes out into the streets naked. But in a strange way, we have to become naked for our shame to die. The moment Adam and Eve fell for the temptation given to them, they made a claim in their minds that they were naked. They had forgotten that they were human and even worse, they forgot who God was. They tried to hide from him. How can you hide from a being like God? You can't. But they forgot. They took matters into their own hands, just like you and me. The things I mentioned before are a fraction of the clothes humans use to hide their shame. I said before that nakedness is a condition that people hate being in. At the very least, it is slightly uncomfortable. Humans were made naked. Humans are born naked. The point I'm making is that we, humans, have forgotten who we are. There are many things, one of which I've already talked about and many that I can't fully explain, that we contribute to our definition of what it means to be human. That is exactly what humanity's problem is. We are humans, how can we define what that means? You can't ask a machine to explain what it is unless the machine was made with the capabilities to do that. We may have rationality, but it wasn't for us to decide who we are. We can make claims about ourselves as much as we want, we are still liars at the end of it all. Let me put it a different way. Names are something given to children. And every name has some kind of story to it. The child who was given that name, does not know that story unless the parents tell it. A child knows nothing about their name besides the fact that it is their name. They can't ask another child or a teacher about their name. They can only ask their parents, the ones who decided that name. How much more do we hardly know anything about ourselves and who we are? Would it not make sense to ask the one who made us who we are? The beautiful thing about that question is that when we ask that question to the right person, we get more than we expected.

So now the statement I made in the previous chapter should make more sense. It may sound like I have no free will, but I actually have more freedom in Christ. In fact, I would argue that anyone who decides who they are based on aspects of humanity, whether physical or not, are the true prisoners. They can march through streets or make declarations to others about themselves, but they are chained around the neck in a field. They can walk wherever they please, just not down that narrow road. I am free to be what I was made to be. Not an author, or an artist, or a prophet, or any title. I am human, plain and simple. And so are you, my dear reader. God declared it, so it should be a statement that makes you joyful. Regardless of how great a talent is, it does not tell the whole story. In fact, it will not make you whole at all. Don't wallow in shame or self-pity if that is you. There is good news. God has come to set the captives free...

My Manhood

In case it wasn't obvious, I'm a man. A Black man specifically. Nothing too crazy about me. I'm strange in my own way but regardless, I'm a fairly average dude. Well...about as average as you can get being crafted in the strange but alluring vision of God, methinks. As a man, I am drawn to many different types of things. If I even start that list I will get into horrifically uncharted territory. But one of those things is strange anomalies in human nature. One of the strange phenomena I've been led to is the ideas of masculinity and femininity. And I'll be honest, I wouldn't blame you if you rolled your eyes at the title of this chapter. Trust me, I had an extensive conversation with God to not let me delve into this topic...how funny our Heavenly Father can be. We came to an agreement that this topic was necessary for the book. There's a good chance that someone will be offended by what I say here. Why would that be the case? It's one of those things that a lot of people hold dear to themselves. You can deny the reality of sexual desire. You can't really do the same for gender. I'm not going to say something like, "I wish it wasn't so difficult." It is true that I wish things were simpler. But humans seem to overcomplicate what is simple. The challenge isn't dissecting men and women. It's stitching them back together.

The first question to ask is one that, at least for this age, is difficult to answer: What are men and women? While it makes no sense, I see why. There are two sides of the gender debate: The Traditionalist view and The Progressive view. The Traditionalist claims that male and female, man and woman, are two points that have no distance between each other. Gender and sex are synonymous terms that practically mean the same thing. There is no way to transition from one to another. You are either one or the other. Masculinity and femininity, in consequence,

60

are traits that are exhibited by the two genders. One is masculine because they do what men typically do and one is feminine because they do what women typically do. Masculine women and feminine men do exist. The two terms I will use for them are tomboy, the woman who has masculine tendencies, and tomgirl, the man who has feminine tendencies. The evidence for this perspective lies within the differences between men and women physically and even psychologically. "Men are more logical and women are more emotional." This difference is what creates gender roles. Men are providers and protectors while women are nurturers and caretakers. The historical basis for this view seems to come from partly European and mostly western history and philosophy. So while other societies might hold different views, they consider this one superior. The Progressive view is a bit more confusing to wrap around. They see gender as a spectrum between the two points of "Man" and "Woman." With this, gender and sex are not synonymous anymore but two different things. Sex refers to biology and what you were born with. The pair of chromosomes that determine whether you are male or female are what is regarded as sex. There is some debate about intersex people but I will not be discussing it. Gender refers to social identification. Your sex can be male but you can be female in gender and vice versa. The idea comes from different cultures throughout history and how men and women performed different tasks throughout those cultures. Masculinity and femininity, then, are not specific but interchangeable. Anyone can be whoever they want regardless of what society says because society is not consistent. There is also another term known as "Non-binary." They exist on the spectrum but wish not to be referred to as one or the other. There isn't so much to say about this that hasn't already been said before. Both the Traditionalist and the Progressive have views of gender ideology that carry some truth with them, which makes choosing between one or the other difficult. That's why I'm not choosing. Instead, I'm going to see what God says. As cliche as it sounds, it makes more sense to see what the creator of man and woman says about them rather than what the creation says. I said before that you can't ask a machine to define what it is, only its creator. If a machine knows what it is, that's because the creator allowed the machine to have that knowledge. We, being a different kind of machine were given bits and pieces of the knowledge about what we are. I believe that the bits of knowledge we have of male and female we have are enough to answer the question. And part of the answer lies in the fact that our personalities, mannerisms, and looks do not make us any less male or female than what you were born as.

That statement might be controversial (I'd be surprised if it wasn't), so I'll give an explanation of what I mean. From the Traditionalist perspective, the two genders have their roles within society. This goes deeper than societal roles and touches on human nature. Our desires, personalities, mannerisms, and looks all contribute to that static binary. Masculinity and femininity are the terms this refers to. (According to society, not Elijah Ellis) Masculine traits are those that are usually more concrete and grounded. Feminine traits are those that are usually more abstract and expressive. It's like a building. Masculine traits would be like the foundation, support, and shape. Feminine traits would be like the design, purpose, and atmosphere. At least, that's just one of many interpretations of what has existed long before the parents of our parents were thoughts ready to be conceived. The most popular concept of what is masculine and feminine comes from Western culture. This isn't to say whether it is right or wrong, rather that it isn't the only one of its kind. Even the more liberal ideas of masculinity and femininity can only capture a mere fraction of that which exists. They might be more accepting of other ways to be human but that's it. The two perspectives of gender, in a weird way, need each other to exist. The Traditionalist needs a comparison to say, "That's wrong," to. The Progressive needs the old ways to say, "No more," to. Obviously, I'm not saying the full truth of what both sides say. I'm saying what I see. The point I'm trying to make right now is that I agree with both, but not in the way you think.

There's an undeniable truth that men and women are different. It doesn't matter what culture you go to, there will be a difference between men and women. I could go into the physical differences like differently shaped pelvises, strength, and bone density. However, I like exploring the weird side of things and that is what I'll do. As of the time of writing this, I go to a university named "Winston Salem State University " (Go rams!). The ratio of females to males is...huge. I'll say it like this: I see the same guys and different girls every time I leave my dorm. Obviously, I'm no omniscient creature, I'm just very observant of my surroundings. That observant nature of mine leads me to listen to conversations. It's not like I care about the subject, but how they talk. Besides slang, people usually use the same sentence structures. But weirdly enough, it was like my subconscious could guess who was male and who was female just from how they talked. There are forms of masculine speech and feminine speech that I could pick up on, but it didn't matter. Even tomgirls who had a very feminine approach to speech had a sense of "maleness" emanating from them. It was a feeling that at the time made no sense to me. I only started recognizing it when I went to college. I told one of my friends this before, that it's like men and women talk differently. "How so," they asked. And I gave the most hesitant, "I have no idea," I ever have. Since then, I stopped caring. Then that same feeling happened again while watching videos of people talking. Whether it be gaming commentary, video essays, or podcasts, there was a distinct nature of men and women. And it then clicked in my head, an idea about men and women: God made them...(duh)

I find it funny now how far the debate on gender has gone. Of course, I understand why it has gone that way. Everyone believes that they have the cure to the sickness of society. The irony is that these people are sick themselves. There has been one constant throughout this chapter and history: Men and women existed. Since the dawn of humanity, there have been males and females. The confusion, then, has nothing to do with what it means to be male and female. In a weird way, humans already know that. The problem is how people want to exist without question of who they are. It seems as if we have to prove who we are to other people in order to exist. I, as a Black man, have to adhere to the ideas of masculinity presented to me by the community I had no choice to be a part of. It seems that way, but really it isn't. We have to prove to ourselves first before we show the world who we are. There is a conflict inside of us that questions who we are. The labels of male and female serve to feed the fire that burns us from the inside. For some, that flame burns hotter than the sun. "I am a man," and "I am a woman," are statements that make our hearts say, "Prove it." Before you know it, you're speaking a certain way, walking with a specific stride, and dressing with clothes to prove the statement you said about yourself. For a while, you feel good about yourself. And then it happens. Someone questions who you are, and the heat of that war starts to come back. That heat manifests itself as fury. "Why can't they accept me?" I've asked myself that question before. God must've decided that I was ready to accept the difficult truth when it comes to this large aspect of many's lives. I had a curious thought within myself after that question: "Why can't you accept yourself?"

The main problem I see with the gender debate is the fact that everyone has to accept what one person says. Sure, there might be a general consensus on what is true for either side of the debate, but on a personal level, things change. You have to accept what one believes about themselves. That's essentially what the entire debate boils down to. The problem comes when we start thinking that our personal beliefs about ourselves apply to others. This doesn't just mean that gender norms are a social construct. It also means that whatever progressive views you have about gender do not need to be followed by another person. By now, you're probably anxious as to what I believe the solution is to gender issues. Simply put, it is acceptance. Not acceptance of your neighbor, but of yourself. This doesn't mean that the thoughts you have about yourself are true. If you are born female, you are female. If you are born male, you are male. Before I continue, I must say that this is not at all easy. Accepting who you are may very well be one of the hardest things to do for you. The reason why, is because the truth is simple. We want to believe we have so much more complexity to our being. Men who believe they have feminine tendencies, women who have masculine tendencies, and those who don't like any of the binary labels. Real love does not entail that you affirm what you feel is true, but accepting that which is true. If you're still not convinced then let me tell you this: I am still in the process of acceptance for myself. If still you are not convinced, then let me tell you how God fits into all of this. Humans are living beings that are fueled by the energy of God. All of that hinges from one simple but explosive fact: He created us. A creator decides what his creation is, not the creation. There's a psalm that expresses reverence for the fact that God knew us while we were forming in our mother's womb. There is also a verse that talks about men and women being made in the "Image of God." I'll talk about that later. Why? Because, I know there is a question that may have been lingering even before this chapter: "Why did God make me like this if he didn't want me to be this way?" It may seem like an easy question, but it isn't. The reason it's so complicated isn't because of God, or even humans. It's because the adversaries of creation. When Adam and Eve took the fruit for themselves, they didn't just make a declaration that they believed they could be like God. They also forfeited the sacred authority they had over the world. Evil soon pervaded what was good. Before I continue, there is a fact about good and evil that you must know: Evil needs good to exist, but good does not need evil to exist. What this means is that evil takes what is good and ruins it. There's more to say about that, but I'll save it for later. I said all of that to say yes, there are many things about you that are good by nature. However, there are also many things about you that are not good. Remember the example I used of a painting splashed with black? That's what I mean. Underneath all of that black paint is a beautiful painting. If you wanted to remove all of the black, then you would simultaneously be destroying what is good. What's interesting about the Christian perspective is that God promised to solve the issue without destroying the canvas. He did this through the person of Jesus.

Jesus showed us what it means to be human, to be who we were made to be. Jesus was one of the most interesting people to be around. He spoke messages that get repeated to this day. He debated against religious leaders about the scriptures they claimed to know and won. He constantly did and said things that perplex people even to this day. Never once did he say what it meant to be a man or woman. All of the sermons and pieces of advice have wisdom that can apply to both genders. One was not considered better than the other. He recognized that men and women, male and female, were made in the image of God. There's this idea that Christianity is inherently sexist. Looking at the surface, it may seem that God sees women as inferior. However, a closer look at scripture reveals the truth of how important women are. In fact, it was women who were blessed with the good news of Christ being resurrected first. Being made in the image of God means that we are to reflect his goodness into the world. What goodness is reflected into the world if we worry about whether or not men or women are speaking, acting, dressing, and being interested in very trivial and useless things? What good does that do to those who are poor in riches and spirit? There is none. Arguing whether or not women should submit to men or if men are supposed to cry only serves that which is evil. And if you are someone who calls themself a Christian and believes anything within those trivial matters, I suggest you really read the gospels and see what Jesus said. Even if there is scripture that says otherwise, remember that there might be some context you are missing. For example, that famous verse that talks about wives submitting to their husbands. That part is true, but many who throw this verse around trying to make women submit to them failed to keep reading. Not many words later it describes what a husband is supposed to do. "Love your wives as Christ loved the church." This doesn't just mean being willing to die for your spouse. The church is the body of believers. Jesus washed the feet of his disciples, who were part of the church that Paul spoke of. At that time, feet were extremely dirty. It was an act of submission. Recognizing the will of the one you serve leads you to serve others. How willing are you, husbands, to wash the feet of your wife? Another thing, any character that is not Christ is not a model for what it means to be human. They are examples of the many different kinds of people within the human condition that God had to work with to pave the way for Christ. He alone is our standard for what it means to be human. No man, no woman, or even personal convictions can tell you how to be that which you have inevitably failed to be. Don't be discouraged, for God will accept you with open arms regardless of who you are. But remember, to accept God means you have to accept yourself, including everything that stained you in life. To accept it means that you understand that it must go away. You have to be transformed. It will inevitably hurt, but the price to pay is nothing compared to the gift of eternal life...

My Judgment

Before I get started with this chapter, I'm going to make a prediction. I have a sneaking suspicion that this will be my most controversial chapter. I know that previously I talked about sexuality, gender ideology, and even how to be the real you. All of which seem to be very sensitive topics in this age. Here's the thing, all I did was put a biblical perspective on what exists. I never made any decisions about how anyone should live their life, only mere assumptions and theories about humanity. There is a huge problem when it comes to these things though. I would be foolish not to admit when something isn't right with the world. Modern sexuality has created a culture of relationships based on objectification. Friends are chosen by attractiveness and not character. Love is decided by lust, and expectations are forced onto the other person in hopes of fulfilling a sexual fantasy. Gender and its many controversies continue to be debated about. The pressures of society make us believe that we have to live within a tight box based on our gender. People are not even considered humans anymore. They are treated according to everything else they are. How to live life is even debated. Everyone has an answer for the questions of existence. Religion is constantly debated. What is true about the divine and its relation to us? Does a divine realm even exist? The existential questions continue to be argued by scholars and normal people. Yet, all of these problems stem from a deeper, darker root: Humans believe that they can make decisions about the world.

Judgment refers to a decision. Usually, it is a decision that decides fate. There's another kind of judgment that I will get to later. What I'll say about it now is that it is not as heavy as a judgment of fate. What I mean by fate is the direction of decisions and consequences.

Here's an example everyone in first world countries can understand: "Christians" tell those who are LGBT+ affiliated that they are going to hell. What makes it judgment is how one believes that they can decide the fate of another. Regardless of who you are, you have judged someone. Whether it be good or bad is besides the point. You and I have made decisions about someone's fate. Now, for the purposes of this chapter, I need to give you another, more forgotten word: Rebuke. To rebuke someone is showing disapproval or criticism for actions or thoughts someone or a group of people make/have. The reason I tell you this is because humans seem to have forgotten the difference between the two and only care about one. We judge what we think we understand. That's why we think we can make certain calls about what others think and even what God thinks. All of those thoughts come together as one singular thought; "I am a good person." I don't mean good as in only morally good. I mean good as in a necessary aspect of existence. Most people don't care to be moral citizens, but good people. Good morals feed the idea of being good. The irony of humanity's judgment is that they do it out of fear. What are they afraid of? It's judgment they fear.

Now I'm going to make another assumption here. There's a good chance that you think I'm a hypocrite for saying everything I did previously. Let me remind you that nothing I say here is a guaranteed truth. Sure, I use evidence from scripture to support my case. But that's the thing, it isn't my word that I believe to be true. It is the scripture I use that has proven itself to be true. My words are that of an average man. There's nothing so remarkable about me that my words should be taken as the ultimate truth. If I gain a following from this book that expects me to give them knowledge, then I have failed as an author and my book deserves to be burned and forgotten by existence itself. I may be knowledgeable, but I am not someone you should put your trust for information in. I, like all humans, have a reason to do what they do. The reason they do it is because of a dogma they possess. Just because an expert says what you agree with does not mean they are right. Any man can take what is true, and suit it for his own benefit. For example, I live in an age where Christianity is being "deconstructed." All of its dogmas and stories are being ripped apart by the masses. People have started thinking about Christianity in the face of logic and have either rejected it altogether or created their own version. Here's the issue, they deconstructed a bastardized Christianity that serves mankind instead of the one it stemmed from. Issues like homosexuality, gender, commandments, morality, and God have been questioned for longer than anyone can imagine. There's a problem when it comes to deconstructing Christianity: Everyone thinks they're right. The Christian that supports homosexuality is judged by those who believe differently. Vice versa, the same is true. Everyone has an interpretation of scripture that they believe to be true. Like I said before, not everyone's interpretation is right. Right interpretation comes with context. The context missing isn't even God, but Christ. If that sounds weird, that's because it is. However, it proves how humans believe that they are better than God. God came as a human and gave us the means to not only be saved, but to be in relationship with him. The context is right there, within the text. But because of human nature, it is disregarded. And the result is a world full of people who believe that their beliefs, no matter how inconsistent, are right.

Was that a bit harsh? Possibly...I never promised to not be harsh. Nothing in this book was made to intentionally offend someone in any kind of way. However, there is an element within any offense taken that proves my point. My words, regardless of what reaction you have, made you consider a certain judgment about me. You could think that God will rebuke me for everything in this book. If he does, then I will accept any judgment he gives. He alone is the only one who can righteously judge me. You could think that God will give me a great reward for offending others. I would question why God would reward me for disrespecting his creation. Or, the judgment I would be most at peace with, you consider this a book that God helped me make. A testimony from a witness of Jesus Christ meant to help others understand the mysteries of God through this strange fellow. Whatever you think about this book, you have made a decision in your heart about it. And for whatever reason, you trust your heart. It may seem like the most logical option to trust yourself. At times, it is true to trust yourself. Like when going to a new restaurant and seeing a dish that you've never heard of, but has familiar elements to it. You will inevitably like it because your heart understands that money is a valuable resource that shouldn't be wasted on huge risks. However, the heart is a lot more complicated than that. In fact, I would echo the words of the prophet Jeremiah and say that it is deceitful above all things and beyond cure. For a while, I couldn't put my fingers on why that was the case. In order to do that, we must explore the heart itself. The heart is an organ in our body that pumps blood to transfer oxygen and other nutrients throughout the body. It works constantly to keep you alive. But we already know about that part. The more interesting part is how we experience what the heart does. The heart is the place where we experience emotions. It's where we feel joy, sadness, heartbreak, fear, anger, and a whole range of other things. I've heard from someone once that the mind and heart are different in how they work. The mind thinks and the heart feels. The mind can be deceived but not the heart. The heart is pure, the mind is corrupt. I disagree with that sentiment. The heart and mind are intertwined with each other. When the heart feels anger, the mind thinks about what it is angry about. When the heart is sad, the mind thinks about what it is sad about. The mind thinks what the heart feels and the heart feels what the mind thinks. There is no start to it, for it is a cycle. I'm no certified psychologist, but I think I can make the assumption that when the body experiences an event of severe impact, both the mind and heart feel, internalize, and rationalize everything about what happened. I'll use a previous example from my life. When my dog died, I started to develop depression. My mind and heart started to become more dead than ever before. My heart could barely feel any joy and my mind could barely think straight. They both agreed on one very specific thing: Suicide. The idea of taking my own life became a growing temptation that plagued my mind almost every single day. The worst part about it, I didn't know how to tell anyone and my body showed no clear signs of it. At any point, my existence would have been gone. And it's difficult to think about how others would feel when you can barely understand yourself. Trying to find a reason to live is a task more difficult than one could imagine. I used to envy those who had a vision brighter than mine. I remember telling someone who claimed to be more spiritually awakened than me that my heart agreed on suicide. They told me that it wasn't my heart, but my mind. Admittedly, I was pissed. Why wouldn't I be? Someone just dismissed my reality of suicidal thoughts because of what they believe. But it became a question that I believe to have a piece of an answer for. More on that later. The point I'm trying to make now is that we are limited in our perspective. Our existence is not one where we can have every answer to every question. The darkness we experience is very much real. I don't deny that people suffer. But to say that you have the answers to the questions of suffering is a bold statement. I would go as far as to say that those who believe they have all the right answers are liars. I've lived long enough to accept the truth that we will never have it all. There will always be something missing from our lives. Now, in order to make the scope of what I'm saying more digestible, let me give you this example: You're taking a class in biology and you learn about evolution. Previously, you were taught that God created the world and everything in it in seven days. The theory of evolution seems to go against a God who made the world in such a short amount of time, right? You then start to believe that God may not be real and science disproves everything about him all the time. Here's the problem: You've failed to understand that story came from an ancient people who knew nothing that you did. You've also failed to realize that our scientific discoveries came thousands of years after that story was made. You've made a judgment about a subject you didn't have enough information about. You missed context that led to a wrong interpretation. Here's the question to ask from that example: What makes you think that you can trust yourself?

Let me add more to that question. You've made promises to people that you have not been consistent with. You've also made promises to yourself that you have broken. Now you may be saying to yourself that it's because we are flawed creatures. And I tell you, yes, we are. Us being imperfect proves that we are incapable of making good judgment about ourselves and the world around us. We put our trust into things that are consistent. Chairs, cars, planes, food, and other things that keep a certain pattern. Even then, there's a chance that these things will fail. A chair can break. Cars and planes can crash, and maybe we added too much salt. But overall, that probability is based on the patterns of these things. We don't keep a pattern, but habits. Habits are behaviors that we have learned over the course of our lifetimes. Our habits activate at moments that make no sense sometimes. What this means is that even the most seemingly consistent things in our lives are inconsistent in nature. So what sense does it make to put so much faith and trust in yourself? We cannot decide the future. We cannot change the past. We can not make any big impact on the present. In a cosmic sense, our impact means nothing. Even the loudest voices of this age will be forgotten in the next. It may be harsh, but even as a Christian I must accept how fleeting and temporary our lives are. Now, this doesn't mean that everyone and everything in the world is not worth putting any trust in. There are trustworthy people in the world. The trust we build with these kinds of people is dependent on how often they can get up when they fall and how sturdy they are before they fall. There is consistency in our inconsistency. It is our beliefs that make us trustworthy. Our core beliefs produce responses, much like growing fruit. Someone who always gets into relationships and blames their partner is not someone you can trust. Someone who blames the world constantly for their circumstances is not someone you can trust. Someone who claims God to be their lord and actively contradicts his word is not someone to be trusted. You get the point. People are untrustworthy when they are hypocrites. Being a hypocrite means you actively go against the values you say you honor. Most people are hypocrites and don't care about it. It doesn't mean you can't change. Hypocrisy becomes its worst if one makes no effort to correct it. Now, here's something interesting about hypocrisy. If you make a choice that goes against your values out of weakness, it is not hypocrisy. For the Christian it would mean this: Sinning followed by repentance. The flesh is weak. Repentance implies a willingness to change your ways. It becomes hypocrisy when the behavior is constant and the person desires no change. So what's my point about all of this? Remember, we're going deeper into how inconsistent humans are. If it seemed like I was jumping around from different topics, it's because I was. Human consistency lies within how inconsistent we are. We brag about being imperfect when we really shouldn't. Is it bad to strive for perfection? Of course not. The only caveat is that there is one perfect man that is your standard. And at this point, you should know who I'm talking about.

But before I get to the good stuff, I have to talk about two things: That lesser judgment and rebuking. I'll start with that lesser judgment. Simply put, it is simple decisions that we make about life. They don't decide fate, but they do give us an idea about something. For example, you see someone help a senior citizen carry groceries. You might think to yourself, "What a nice person they are." It's true that they are being nice at that moment. Another example is if I saw a woman I found attractive. I would say, "What a pretty woman." Or if I'm being realistic, "She kinda bad." I brought this up because there might be someone slightly confused at what I am saying. Don't think too much about this form of judgment, it's mostly harmless. It can lead to more powerful judgments if not kept in check. It really just boils down to this: Be mindful that the person you look at has a story you don't know. Now for the concept of rebuking: It is equally as important as judgment because the two get mistaken. If you need a refresher on what that is, it's expressing disapproval of someone's thoughts or actions. This is what I believe we should do. Several parts in the Bible command people to rebuke your brother, neighbor, or friend. "Why must we rebuke others?" "Should we not let them live their lives?" I'm sure that the task of rebuking someone, especially in this age, is questioned. Well, as usual, I have an extended answer to this question. It requires us to explore morality for a bit.

Let me ask you this question: Is it right to let someone you know abuse another person? For example, if you have a relative that abuses their partner, is it right to let them continue, especially when you can do something about it? The answer to that question opens up one kind of human morality. It is the behavior towards another human. There is some complexity to this, but for the sake of argument we will only focus on the more broad idea. So, what do I mean by behavior for another human? Pretty much, exactly what the phrase is. What actions do you take for or against another person? Now, at least in America within the age this book is released, the general basis for this behavior echoes the words of Jesus himself. "Treat others how you want to be treated." Essentially, be kind to people. There's a reason to do this and unfortunately, people have twisted the idea for themselves. There is a very selfish motive for doing this that many cannot see themselves doing. It's because of the second part of that phrase: "...how you want to be treated." There's benefit to be had when treating another human with respect. Whether it be something small like mutual respect or something greater like a lifelong friend/partner, there's something to be gained. However, that isn't how life works. Life is a lot more unfair than we like to admit. So what real reason do we have to be kind to other humans? Simply because they are. If you follow the Christian worldview, you know exactly what I'm about to say. I've already established before that humans, regardless of who they are, are created beings. This means a lot more than what the words imply. For an artist to create a drawing or an architect to create a building, a certain amount of all of you is needed. Creation requires time, will, and purpose. Creations of man that are made with all of these in mind are considered things that have a lot of "soul" put into them. How much more precious are humans? They are sacred beings with a divine purpose. We are created to experience the goodness and love of God and his creation. Then we spread that goodness into the world he created. That is the purpose which we drove ourselves away from. Here's the thing, Adam and Eve didn't stop being human when they sinned. They developed and passed down all of the consequences of sin and its power to drag creation back into the darkness. If humans were not valuable, why did God put so much effort into giving them a way to be saved? Why would he sacrifice his only son to be the ultimate sacrifice for humanity's collective sin? There's a price that has to be paid for our salvation. If there is intrinsic value in all humans, do all humans not deserve some kind of action taken towards them that guarantees their wellbeing? Now, here's the caveat behind that "wellbeing" word: It does not mean kissing ass. Wellbeing and desire are two different things. Oftentimes, we do that which is not good for us but feels good. It takes a good amount of effort to do what is actually good for us. Likewise, it takes a lot to consider the wellbeing of another human. People think it's easy. I think it's not. Maybe I'm just a bad person. Or maybe people are liars. Personally, if God were to tell me to talk to any acquaintances or friends that are gay that their lifestyle is not fit for the kingdom, I would need time to consider the setting and what to say. I know that deep down, there is an urge to do what is right. But at the same time, there is a powerful urge to just let them be happy. But how content would I be when God tells me that I failed his task. Sure, God won't stop chasing that person even if I fail as his channel. But to think that I would consider what is desirable instead of what is good in that moment would leave me with regret. Let me make it clear that it isn't just homosexuality that I have that sentiment for. People who drink, smoke, sleep around, get into constant relationships or really just whatever they do. In a way, it seems like their lives are happy, so why should I bother? This leads me to the next subject of morality: How to treat yourself.

This won't be long. Mainly because I already discussed a good portion of everything I need here. To summarize, humans are inconsistent creatures whose actions prove themselves untrustworthy. Paradoxically, we understand ourselves the most and the least. We know who we are by name. We know how we feel. We know what we like. On the other side of that coin, we don't know who we are as humans. We don't know what these feelings truly mean to us. We don't know how to truly experience what we like and desire. Treating yourself right does not mean catering to every desire. It means serving our wellbeing with love. There may be a voice in your head telling you to think and do certain things. That voice is inconsistent with reality. Even if the voice makes a good point. The most broad example is discipline. We have a desire to be disciplined, but we would rather sleep at crap times and wake up feeling depressed and exhausted as if we never slept the night before. The more specific examples are those which I already discussed before. It may be hard to resist the urge to stay in bed, but you must get up. It may be hard to resist explosive anger, but you must keep yourself at peace. It may be hard to resist lust, but you must not let your heart be swayed. From this Christian's perspective, it is one of the hardest things I have to do every day. The action for me is not the hardest part, it is recovering from a fall. To recognize that you are violating the sacred order of the one who created you is already disheartening enough. But how does one come back when they have failed so much? The answer lies in the fact that there is nothing we can do. We say not to judge others. So why do we judge ourselves so much? I have no answer besides what I already said. The solution, then, is not anything in our nature. Rather, it is in the nature of God himself, who sent his son down for us. He alone is able to judge us because he is God, but he never judged anyone while here.

I don't think I have to say much here. He didn't come to condemn the world, but to save it. Jesus had all rights to judge and to condemn, but he never did. Humans are quite frail if you think about it. No matter how much strength you have, or how smart you are, or how big your army is, one bullet can end someone's life. Even in an emotional sense, people are fragile. They will let you say anything except for what they hate. That is when you will see them break. The weight of the world they carry crushes their shoulders and the pain of sticks, stones, and guns can be lethal. Isn't funny how someone like Jesus carried all of that on the cross. We don't give much credit to what Jesus has done. We say, "He died for your sins," and never go any further. He didn't just die for our sins. He died to take our place for the punishment we deserve. He died to conquer death itself. He died to break the cosmic chains of a universe locked in a dance of death and despair. He didn't just die for our sins. He became sin itself and killed it. And this story would've been a tragedy if Jesus did not rise from the dead. This did something for the world. It didn't end every last bit of evil in the world. But it kickstarted a process to where all of creation will be healed. And that healing starts with us humans. Our nature meant that we were separated from God, and his goodness was like poison to us. There used to be mediators for God and men. Now, the ultimate mediator has paved the way for anyone, regardless of who they are, to experience the goodness and glory of God. What does this have to do with judgment? I'm trying to say that we have no good reason to judge anyone for what they do since we are all imprisoned by sin. Rebuking is something Christians are supposed to do in order to show others that what they do is wrong. There is a better way, the first step is Jesus. Everything that comes after is a lifelong process that leads you to being more like him. God wants everyone. You don't have to look at the next person and think, "What a great Christian they are." Christianity is not about comparison. It is about God and humanity. Humans, who are creatures made in the image of God, could never be like him. Yet, God gave them the opportunity to be with him. If you believe that none of this answers anything about judgment, I would ask you to reconsider the decisions you have made about the world and this chapter first...

Who Is The Loser?

Everyone believes themselves to be something greater than another. I'm no exception. While I considered myself a loser in many ways, I did have my pride. It is true that at the time of writing this that I: have had no experiences with women in any kind of way, have never been to any crazy parties, have failed classes, have proven how lazy I can be, and a whole list of other things. What I find interesting is that I'm not the only one. Comparison is the antithesis of growth. A flower cannot be like the others. Though it may share similarities, it is its own flower with its own petals, leaves, and stem. Ever since I gave my life to Christ, I've become observant of other people. Where there was jealousy, there was a story I never knew. And from the stories I've heard, one thing was made clear: Everyone is a loser.

If I were to make a list, you would be on there somewhere. But the list would be way too long. So instead, I will spare your time and give you some of the broad categories. They include: Men, women, old, young, rich, poor, gay, straight, cisgender, transgender, leaders, followers, promiscuous, cellibate, wise, and foolish.

Keep this in mind, I only scratched the surface of the kinds of humans that exist. But I'm sure you get the point. Regardless of who you are reading this, you fit into one of these categories. The reason is not something that you should feel guilty for. The reason is this: You have tried to find life in something that wasn't God. The consequence was that you lost it. Loser entails that you lost something. Everyone has lost their life. The proof is that everyone is doomed to die. Most people experience a void inside of them. A bottomless pit of fulfillment that continues to fester in the heart. Some have made themselves numb to it by experiencing the pleasures of this world. Things like money, sex, drugs, career, purpose, love, and spirituality among other things. However a lot of us do not get that luxury. We are reminded of the void. Whether it be heartbreak from death or romance, depression, or boredom. What's funny is that even now, I still have issues with that. There is a constant anxiety caressing my neck for every word I write here. It tells me that writing this will only make me more unpopular because I'll offend someone, or that no one will care, or no one will understand me. Well, as you can see, I didn't submit to it. One of the most important lessons that I have to teach myself constantly is that regardless of how this life goes, in new creation, I will have something better. If I don't get married in this life, or become successful, or die without anyone knowing, I will have left a great mark on the world. That mark is a body that will be resurrected in the last days to experience God's full glory. If I start thinking about whether I'll be married in heaven, I'll lose sight of the one who made it. If I start thinking about success as a result of God, I will lose sight of that which is already good. If I think about how well known I am, I will lose sight of the greatest relationship I have. With God, there is no losing. This doesn't mean prosperity or generational wealth. It means riches beyond human conception. It may be disappointing to hear that, but this world and everything in it will pass away. The only thing that will remain is the word of God. If you call yourself a Christian and continue to live according to the world, whether it be sexuality, or purpose, or drugs, or whatever else, sinful or not, I have a challenge for you: Let every bit of it go. If you smoke, or if you're in a relationship, or if you sleep around, or if you drink to get drunk, or if you miss the old days, or if you have no idea what's next, let it go. Take one long deep breath and imagine the past you had, now exhale every bit of it out. You don't lose with God. There is no shame to be had in what you are. The point isn't to fix it yourself. It's to let him fix you. Does one have to be clean to take a shower? Likewise, why do you think you need to be in a certain condition for God to love you? I wasn't scared of death before.

Mainly because I saw it as a means to end my suffering, so I figured that death should have its way. I don't fear death now because I know that regardless, God is still sovereign over it all. I am confident in where I am going. And you should be confident as well. Not because of anything you or I have done. It is God alone who has done and is still doing the work. If you aren't a Christian, for whatever reason, I would ask that you read the next chapter. Even if you are a Christian, I'm sure it'll help you understand something.

What Is It?

What even is the gospel that I've been hinting at since the beginning of this book? I have to warn you, it isn't complicated. There is a very intricate story behind it, but even a child could understand. Be wary of those who present a truth that is complicated in nature. They only care for themselves. I'll start by giving my explanation of the gospel and then I'll give the story behind it.

The gospel is simply this: "God, the creator of the universe loves you and wants to be in relationship with you. There is an interference to this relationship called sin. However, through the person of Jesus, who is God incarnated as a human, he has provided the means to be in relationship with him through his life, death, and resurrection. The path to eternal life, knowing and trusting God, has been paved for all who choose to believe." This is how I give the gospel. Same message, different words. Now here's the story behind that gospel:

"In the beginning was a being full of love and power. He never needed creation, for he was three. All three were one, but not each other. For whatever reason, he decided to create life from nothing. Not just the living parts of it, but everything. From the stars in the sky to the atoms of the dirt. The universe and its vastness were created by him. The pinnacle of creation was mankind. Man and woman, created in his image to reflect his goodness into the earth. Everything was good, until that deceiver came. For some vile reason, a being created by God wanted to become what God is. He twisted the truth to convince man and woman to join him in his quest for rebellion. At first, they were reluctant. But they were convinced that they could seize power by their own strength. The first sin was born...and from it, all of creation was introduced to evil. They told God with their hearts to step away...and he did, respecting their request. But God was not done with them. From the moment they sinned, he was on a mission to save all of his creation. God was faced with the challenge that is the human heart. The human heart was in rebellion against its creator. All things good were ruined. Life was doomed to die. People would hunger and thirst no matter how much they ate or drank. People would violate the goodness of humanity that remained through all kinds of atrocities. Kings and queens of different nations would force those they hated to live a life not deserved. Even those who ate the dirt ruined that which was good amongst themselves. The human heart was never satisfied with anything. It always wanted to be right. It drank poison and longed for a cure while drinking. Every single day was another atrocity committed by someone against another or themselves. A heartbroken father, full of love, had to watch its own creation that he loved so much be consumed by evil. But he would not give up. He chose a man named Abraham. He was the catalyst for the reaction that would occur later on. God promised this man that he would have children that outnumbered the stars, despite the old age of him and his wife, Sarah. This man would have many moments of weakness and evil within him. But he still had faith in God. God, being a man of his word, kept his promise to Abraham throughout it all and gave him a son. When the child was born, Abraham and Sarah were both happy. God then tested the faith of Abraham by making him sacrifice his only son. Abraham's faith would prove great, and he would keep his son as God stopped Abraham and provided another sacrifice. His son, Isaac, had two sons. The youngest of these sons, Jacob, would have 12 sons that would become a nation called Israel. This nation would become enslaved by Egyptians. God, being slow to anger, finally decided that Egypt had done enough and did not want to repent. So he chose Moses to free the Israelites. The Israelites decided to give their lives up to this god that freed them. But they proved that they were just like the other humans, worshiping an idol in God's place. From this, the law was born. 613 commands given to a people with hardened hearts to follow. It was a temporary solution to a long-lasting problem. Even with this law, Israel proved themselves to be just as evil and twisted as the nations around them. The same grotesque atrocities committed by surrounding nations were done by these chosen people. God declared them guilty, just like the rest. But even though they were as rotten as the rest, God still made a way. Despite the madness, there was a faithful remnant. Through a specific bloodline a man would be born and save humanity. This was a promise continued from the first man, Adam, and the first woman, Eve. The prophets spoke of this savior and the suffering he would endure. But those who heard them, did not listen. But those who listened, waited. They waited even when death kissed their cheeks. But their wait was not in vain. From a virgin, a man would be born. This man was named Jesus. He was sent to confront the power of evil that enslaved all of creation. He healed many and performed miracles. He taught many a way of life that was completely different from what was believed in that day. He loved everyone and showed them the mercy that was presented by God. There was not an ounce of evil within him. He did not ever affirm the evil within others, no matter how close he was to someone. He showed them how to live. But this was not all that he did. He suffered in all kinds of ways. He was tempted by The Devil himself, seeing all that temptation had to offer. He suffered through poverty, seeing the drought that all had suffered. He was hated by his own people for wanting them to be true to the words they spoke. He was even left to die by his closest friends, for they all denied knowing him. He suffered the entirety of what evil had. From both man and spirit he was killed. Everyone believed that it was over...that he was gone forever. But even in death, he was not finished. He brought all that evil offered to death and defeated it. He then rose from the dead, from the power of God and his love. Being the only begotten Son of God, he accomplished what no man could do. And from this resurrection was a new path introduced. The path to eternal life was accessible to all kinds of people. No matter who you are, you have the choice to be freed from all that evil brings. Those who truly believed in their hearts in the name of Christ and confessed with their mouths the sins they have done are not only forgiven, but have a name within the book of life. They have a spot in eternity with God."

The gospel that I have spoken throughout this collection of thoughts is good beyond measure. It is more than just saying God exists. It is more than saying what is right and wrong. It is more than going to church on sundays. It is more than just saying "God is good." It is the manifestation of God's goodness. It is a life-changing power that brings joy and peace in a world full of evil and suffering. It fills a void that nothing on earth can. Things of this world can only feed the void in all of our hearts. God is the only one who can fill it up forever. Christ has lived a life that no one else could ever live. He was sinless, and he died as one, bringing it to the grave. But praise God, he has risen from the dead. When you accept Christ, he stands in your place. And through a process called sanctification, you become more like him. His spirit dwells within us, making us holy every day. It is not exclusive to those who consider themselves righteous. It is for sinners like me and you to be reconciled with God. It is not a piece of joy, but the entirety of it. When you accept God into your heart, he walks beside you. He is with you every step of your journey, guiding you to the right direction. Whatever risks are involved are a test of your faith. God loves a free heart that loves freely. Not a heart that loves what it does not know or a heart forced to love. He calls all kinds of people every single day, hoping they will make the right choice: The one full of tattoos, the prostitute, the addicted, the lonely, the homosexual, the criminal, the poor, the rich, the lame, everyone. Or as I would say: The Losers.

The gospel is not an excuse to sin, for we are free from that. Anyone who says, "God will forgive me," or "God knows my heart," is a deceiver to themselves and others. They serve an idol that says that they can live however they want. The gospel is not just about heaven, for even Jesus said that will pass away. Anyone who condemns anyone to hell is one who serves a self-righteous heart. Hell exists and is not desirable. But if the main point of the gospel was about hell, I believe there would be way more of a description of it. Any gospel that preaches anything apart from Jesus giving us the opportunity to be saved from our sins is not the gospel. There is no other gospel. Any pastor who preaches a word that doesn't call Jesus God is a false teacher. The selling point of the gospel is Jesus, not us. Though we are important, nothing we do could ever compare to the sacrifice of Jesus, who told the Heavenly Father to forgive them even as he died.

I'm no one great and I don't wish to be. I'm not perfect in any sense of the matter. I lived a life of sin and as of the time writing this, I've only known God for about two-and-a-half years. I still have my issues. I still long for other things like a relationship, or money, or confidence, or strength. I'm still kind of new to this business, so why am I doing this? Why am I speaking about issues I have no experience in or about a gospel that I haven't studied as much as those who have put their lives into it? There are two answers to this question: My answer and God's answer. One says that he told me to do it. The other says that there is more to life than experience. Wisdom is not taught through experience but the understanding of it. By some miracle, I was given a heart that is willing to listen, no matter how much I want to speak. And because I have this new heart, I can see more than just the experience. Even when I hear someone say they are ok with my ears, my heart hears pain. It hears tears that were never given the space to cry, much like mine. It hears a barrier that shields itself from trusting other people because of broken promises. I'm not writing this as some proof that God exists. Most people already know that he exists. I was not to write an argument for God, for others already have done that. I am here to be the reaching hand of God. And the words I was afraid of saying have made themselves known to those who find this book.

A big part of that fear has to do with the deconstruction of Christianity. I believed that too many people were already succumbing to this destruction. But I realized that this deconstruction proved God's goodness. Through the hearts of men, women, and even children, the false gospels are being destroyed. It wasn't the end. It was the means to a new beginning. God is not so weak that the thoughts of mere mortals that he made could defeat him. Their evil was turned into a means for Christianity to be reconstructed. I am just one of the many proofs of that reconstruction. Whatever I was before, is gone. I used to think that God would fix my inner child. Many are like me, seeking to have their inner child healed. I realized now that wishing for that inner child meant I was wishing for my sinful nature to become innocent again. I'm glad that desire is dead. If God answered my request, I would relive every suffering again. But I am made new and better than what I could ever be. But I couldn't do it alone.

To those who do read this, know that you have made an impact in my life. Whether you are family, friends, enemies, or that wife that I wanted and finally found, God used you to change me. You know who you are, for any that know me. And for those that don't, you know a piece of my life that I repressed for a long time. And maybe one day, I'll be able to do what this book does but with my actual voice. Or maybe I'll just continue to write (wink wink). At this point I don't know what else to say. I said at first that this was an apology to God. But now that I am here, at the end, all I can do is be grateful for everything he has done for me. Whether or not it has made itself known now or will make itself known later. I know that the promises that God gave me will come to pass...